Invitation to a Journey

A Road Map for Spiritual Formation

M. Robert Mulholland Jr.

INTERVARSITY PRESS
DOWNERS GROVE, ILLINOIS 60515

InterVarsity Press® is the book-publishing division of InterVarsity Christian Fellowship®, a student movement active on campus at hundreds of universities, colleges and schools of nursing in the United States of America, and a member movement of the International Fellowship of Evangelical Students. For information about local and regional activities, write Public Relations Dept., InterVarsity Christian Fellowship, 6400 Schroeder Rd., P.O. Box 7895, Madison, WI 53707-7895.

New Testament quotations, unless otherwise noted, are the author's own translation. Old Testament quotations, unless otherwise noted, are from the Revised Standard Version of the Bible, copyright 1946, 1952, 1971 by the Division of Christian Education of the National Council of the Churches of Christ in the U.S.A. and are used by permission.

Cover illustration: Roberta Polfus

ISBN 0-8308-1386-1

Printed in the United States of America ∞

Library of Congress Cataloging-in-Publication Data
Mulholland, M. Robert.
  Invitation to a journey: a road map for spiritual formation/M.
Robert Mulholland.
    p.   cm.
  Includes bibliographical references.
  ISBN 0-8308-1386-1
  1. Spiritual formation.   I. Title.
BV4501.2.M74   1993
248—dc20   93-3529
                                                                          CIP

17   16   15   14   13   12
06   05   04   03

To
Darrell
John
Steve
Steve
brothers
in Christ
and
God's nurturing
community

Acknowledgments ————————————————— 9

Prologue —————————————————————— 11

Part I The Road Map: The Nature of Spiritual Formation — 15

1 The Process ——————————————————— 19

2 Being Conformed ————————————————— 25

3 The Image of Christ ————————————————— 33

4 For the Sake of Others ——————————————— 40

Part II The Vehicle: Personality and Piety ————————— 45

5 Creation Gifts ——————————————————— 49

6 One-Sided Spirituality ——————————————— 57

7 Holistic Spirituality ———————————————— 64

Part III The Journey: Spiritual Disciplines ————————— 75

8 The Classical Christian Pilgrimage ————————— 79

9 Classical Spiritual Disciplines ——————————— 102

10 The Nature of the Spiritual Disciplines ——————— 120

11 The Inner Dynamics of the Spiritual Disciplines ——— 135

Part IV Companions on the Way: Corporate and Social
Spirituality———————————————————141

12 Corporate Spirituality ——————————————— 143

13 Social Spirituality ————————————————— 158

Notes ——————————————————————— 169

Acknowledgments

The essence of this book was developed as a retreat for the ordained and diaconal ministers of the Virginia Annual Conference of the United Methodist Church. My thanks to Bishop Thomas Stockton for the privilege of that ministry.

Thanks are also due to Dr. David L. McKenna, President of Asbury Theological Seminary, and to the Board of Trustees, who granted me a sabbatical leave from my administrative responsibilities in order to complete this manuscript.

A special word of thanks to Rodney Clapp, editor for InterVarsity Press, who patiently understood when administrative pressures precluded the completion of the manuscript by the original deadline, who worked faithfully and diligently with me on the manuscript during its development, and who was an encouragement and support during the writing process.

Most of all, I am once again deeply grateful to my family, who bore with my absences as I developed this manuscript. They are my primary spiritual formation community, and without them this book would be far less than it is.

Prologue

Spiritual formation has become one of the major movements of the late twentieth century. Spiritualities of all varieties have emerged upon the landscape of our culture—Hindu, Buddhist, Muslim, Zen, various Eastern meditation techniques, New Age spirituality and a confusing welter of cults, to say nothing of chemically induced alterations of consciousness. In the face of a radical loss of meaning, value and purpose engendered by a largely materialistic, hedonistic, consumer society, human hearts are hungering for deeper realities in which their fragmented lives can find some measure of wholeness and integrity, deeper experiences with God through which their troubled lives can find meaning, value, purpose and identity.

The Christian community, which should have been a clear voice of liberation and wholeness in the wilderness of human bondage and brokenness, has too often been merely an echo of the culture, further confusing those on a wandering and haphazard quest for wholeness. A multitude of Christian "gurus" have emerged who promise their followers life, liberty and the perfection of happiness. Superficial pop spiritualities abound, promising heaven on earth but producing only failure and frustration for those genuinely hungering and thirsting after God.

Perhaps such a failed or frustrated quest is what has brought you to this book. I pray that you will find here not another quick journey down a dead-end road, but an invitation to step through the narrow gate onto the difficult road of the classic Christian journey toward wholeness in Christ.

I do not know what your perception of Christian discipleship might be, but much contemporary Christian spirituality tends to view the spiritual life as a static possession rather than a dynamic and ever-developing growth toward wholeness in the image of Christ. When spirituality is viewed as a static possession, the way to spiritual wholeness is seen as the acquisition of information and techniques that enable us to gain possession of the desired state of spirituality. Discipleship is perceived as "my" spiritual life and tends to be defined by actions that ensure its possession. Thus the endless quest for techniques, methods, programs by which we hope to "achieve" spiritual fulfillment. The hidden premise behind all of this is the unquestioned assumption that we alone are in control of our spirituality. In brief, we assume we are in control of our relationship with God.

When spirituality is viewed as a journey, however, the way to spiritual wholeness is seen to lie in an increasingly faithful response to the One whose purpose shapes our path, whose grace redeems our detours, whose power liberates us from crippling bondages of the prior journey and whose transforming presence meets us at each turn in the road. In other words, holistic spirituality is a pilgrimage of deepening responsiveness to God's control of our life and being.

Let me briefly sketch for you where we will be going together in this book. In the first section, "The Road Map: The Nature of Spiritual Formation," I want to share with you what may appear to be a rather simplistic definition of spiritual formation: *Spiritual formation is a process of being conformed to the image of Christ for the sake of others.* Upon closer examination, however, you will discover that this definition encompasses the essential dynamics of spiritual formation and effectively counters cultural dynamics that work against holistic spirituality.

In the second section, "The Vehicle: Personality and Piety," I will share with you some insights on the integration of personality and spiritual formation. Too often spiritual formation is seen as something "added on" to our personality that solves all our emotional, psychological, physical and mental problems. When this happens, potentially serious emotional, psychological, physical or mental problems can be repressed or covered over with a veneer of "spirituality" that claims to solve the problem. In such instances, persons are often told, "You just need to pray more, go to church more, read your Bible more, be more obedient to God, deal with unconfessed sin in your life, and everything will be fine." This is like telling persons with broken legs that they just need to run more and strengthen the muscles. Our spirituality is not an "add-on," it is the very essence of our being. We are spiritual beings whose emotions, psychology, body and mind are the incarnation of our spiritual life in the world. We will see that holistic spirituality always takes place in the midst of our emotional, psychological, physical and mental conditions and emerges out of them.

We will also see in part two that in holistic spirituality any "one-size-fits-all" prescription is not realistic. We are unique persons, and our relationship with God always manifests that individuality. Our process of spiritual formation toward wholeness may be very different from others'.

In the third section, "The Journey: Spiritual Disciplines," we will think together about the nature of spiritual disciplines. Here we will consider not only the classical disciplines of the Christian tradition such as prayer, spiritual reading and liturgy (which in its broad sense is related not only to worship but also to daily office, fasting, study, retreat) but also, and particularly, those very individualized spiritual disciplines that the Spirit of God brings into our lives to shape us in the image of Christ.

In the final section, "Companions on the Way: Corporate and Social Spirituality," we will conclude with the corporate and social dimensions of spiritual formation, an aspect that is frequently missed in the faddishness of spiritual formation these days. As John Wesley constantly emphasized, there can be no personal holiness without social holiness. Much of what passes for spiritual formation these days is a very privatized, individualized experience. It does not enliven and enrich the body of Christ, nor is it vitally dependent upon the body of Christ for its own wholeness. Neither does it play itself out in the dynamics of life in the world. It doesn't bring the reality of relationship with God and Jesus Christ to bear upon the brokenness and the pain in the world around us. Thus corporate and social spirituality is an essential part of our holistic spiritual formation.

Part I

The Road Map:

The Nature of Spiritual Formation

There are many definitions of spiritual formation. Some call for unquestioned and absolute obedience to a leader or a ruling group (observe the extreme consequences of this in the tragedy of David Koresh and his followers). Some call for certain "evidences" that are believed to confirm one's spirituality (such as speaking in tongues or handling snakes). Some promise plenty and prosperity to those who fulfill certain requirements. Some consist of dos and don'ts. Some seem to allow almost any behavior as part of their spirituality.

How does one select from such a welter of options? Perhaps *selection* is not the correct step. It may be better for me to develop a working definition of spiritual formation that has integrity with the scriptural witness to life in relationship with God, and let you work out its relationship to whatever other definition of spiritual formation you may have adopted.

In this section we will develop a fourfold definition of spiritual formation as (1) a process (2) of being conformed (3) to the image of Christ (4) for the sake of others.

Scripture is quite clear in its insistence that we have fallen short of God's purposes for our creation. It is equally clear in its revelation that God works graciously through all the aspects of human life to bring us to the fulfillment of God's will for our wholeness. Thus spiritual formation is a process of involvement with God's gracious work. But spiritual formation as a process will be seen to move against the grain of our instant-gratification culture and the possessiveness of an acquisitive society. Once we understand spiritual formation as a process, all of life becomes spiritual formation. Cooperation with God's gracious work moves us toward the wholeness of Christ. Rebellion against God's gracious work moves us into destructive and dehumanizing emptiness, into increasingly dysfunctional lives that are self-destructive and treat others as objects to be manipulated and used for our own purposes.

Scripture is also clear in its witness to the fact that only God can liberate us from our bondage, heal our brokenness, cleanse us from our uncleanness and bring Life out of our deadness. We cannot do it by ourselves. Thus spiritual formation is the experience of being shaped by God toward wholeness. But spiritual formation as "being conformed" will also be seen to move against the grain of our do-it-yourself culture and our powerful need to be in control of our existence. Generally, we like to lift ourselves up by our own bootstraps. Self-reliance is deeply ingrained in us. To allow someone else to control our life is seen as weakness, to be avoided at all costs. The English poet William Henley captured the spirit of our culture well when he wrote, "I am the master of my fate, I am the captain of my soul."[1] But spiritual formation as "being conformed" will reveal that *God* is the initiator of our growth toward wholeness and we are to be pliable clay in God's hand.

Scripture reveals from the very beginning that human wholeness is associated with the image of God. We are created in the image of God (Gen 1:26-27). The New Testament parallel to this is that we are to become the likeness of Christ (2 Cor 3:18), who is "the image of the invisible God" (Col 1:15). Spiritual formation in the image of Christ will also be seen to move against the grain of our self-actualization culture and prevailing perspectives which tend to create God in our image. The image of Christ will be seen as the ultimate reality of human wholeness, the consummation for which each heart longs. It will, however, also be seen to be cruciform in the essence of its nature; a dying is involved in our growth toward wholeness, a cross upon which we lose our old self with its bondages and brokennesses.

Finally, Scripture reveals that human wholeness is always actualized in nurturing one another toward wholeness, whether within the covenant community of God's people or in the role of God's people in healing brokenness and injustice in the world. Spiritual formation "for the sake of others" will be seen to move against the grain of a privatized and individualized religion and the deep-seated belief that spiritual life is a matter between the individual and God. There can be no wholeness in the image of Christ which is not incarnate in our relationships with others, both in the body of Christ and in the world.

Chapter 1
The Process

Gracious and loving God, you know the deep inner patterns
of my life that keep me from being totally yours. You know the
misformed structures of my being that hold me in bondage to
something less than your high purpose for my life. You also know
my reluctance to let you have your way with me in these areas.
Hear the deeper cry of my heart for wholeness and by your grace
enable me to be open to your transforming presence in
this reading. Lord, have mercy.

When we say that the Christian journey is a *process*, we express
a truth that is both well-known and well-nigh unknown at the same
time. If you ask most Christians about their spiritual pilgrimage,
they will say that it is a day-by-day experience with its ups and
downs, its victories and defeats, its successes and failures. In brief,
it is a process. But if you were to ask them how God works transformation in their lives, many would indicate that God "zaps" them
at some point and instantly changes them. How often Christians
struggle to create the setting in which God can "zap" them out of
their brokenness and into wholeness!

We live in an instant-gratification culture. Just sit near a vending
machine and watch what happens when people do not get the product they have paid for. They will begin to complain to anyone handy

or even begin to abuse the machine. This silly example illustrates a deeper dimension of our culture. We have generally come to expect immediate returns on our investments of time and resources. If we have a need, we have only to find the right place, product or procedure and invest the right amount of time, energy and resources, and our need will be met. It is not surprising that we, as members of an instant-gratification culture, tend to become impatient with any process of development that requires of us more than a limited involvement of our time and energies. If we do not receive the desired results almost instantly, we become impatient and frustrated.

Often our spiritual quest becomes a search for the right technique, the proper method, the perfect program that can immediately deliver the desired results of spiritual maturity and wholeness. Or we try to create the atmosphere for the "right" spiritual moment, that "perfect" setting in which God can touch us into instantaneous wholeness. If only we can find the right trick, the right book or the right guru, go to the right retreat, hear the right sermon, instantly we will be transformed into a new person at a new level of spirituality and wholeness. Kenneth Leech, a leading Anglican writer in spirituality, sums up the situation well:

> In the years since the 1960's we have seen "the popular unfolding of an authentically spiritual quest. . . ." Yet linked with this search for authentic experiential knowledge of God and of "inner space" there has been a narrowing of vision, a desire for instant ecstasy, instant salvation. . . . It is the quest for the correct method, the right mantra, the short cut which brings insight, which has marked so much of the recent spiritual undergrowth.[1]

It is not that right techniques, right methods and right programs are not beneficial. Nor should we minimize the importance of transforming spiritual moments on our pilgrimage. All these are important. But there is something about the nature of spiritual wholeness and the growth toward that wholeness that is very much a process.

The Reality of Process

Spiritual growth is, in large measure, patterned on the nature of physical growth. We do not expect to put an infant into its crib at night and in the morning find a child, an adolescent or yet an adult. We expect that infant to grow into maturity according to the processes that God has ordained for physical growth to wholeness. The same thing is true of our spiritual life.

Yes, there are spurts of growth in our spiritual development. A few years ago I had a little boy. Then, within a year, he became a man. He went through one of those adolescent growth spurts. He grew almost a foot in height, his voice dropped into a deep bass, he began to shave, his body filled out—he was a different person. The same thing happens in our spiritual life. For a while we may live on a plateau of life and relationship with God. Then one of those moments comes in which we experience a growth spurt and find ourselves on a new level of life and relationship with God. We experience God in a new and different way. We see ourselves and life in a new perspective. Old things pass away, and new things take their place. But if we mistake such a growth spurt for all there is in spirituality, then we are not prepared for the long haul toward spiritual wholeness. We will tend to languish as we wait for another spurt to come along. Or we will try to reproduce the setting in which the previous spurt took place, hoping to create another such experience.

What we don't realize is that often a period of apparent spiritual stagnation, a time in which we don't feel as if we are going anywhere, a phase of life in which our relationship with God seems weak or nonexistent, the time of dryness, of darkness—what the mothers and fathers of the church speak of as the desert experience—is filled with nurturing down below the surface that we never see. The great Scottish Christian novelist George MacDonald puts it this way:

To give us the spiritual gift we desire, God may have to begin far back in our spirit, in regions unknown to us, and do much work that we can be aware of only in the results. . . . In the gulf of our unknown being God works behind our consciousness. With His holy influence, with His own presence, . . . He may be approaching our consciousness from behind, coming forward through regions of our darkness into our light, long before we begin to be aware that He is answering our request—has answered it, and is visiting His child.[2]

Or, as the seventeenth-century French spiritual writer François Fénelon says, "God hides his work, in the spiritual order as in the natural order under an unnoticeable sequence of events."[3]

This hidden work of God is a nurturing that prepares us for what appears to be a quantum leap forward. What we see as the quantum leap may actually be only the smallest part of what has been going on in a long, steady process of grace, working far beyond our knowing and understanding, to bring us to that point where we are ready for God to move us into a new level of spiritual awareness and a new depth of wholeness in relationship with God in Christ. There simply is no instantaneous event of putting your quarter in the slot and seeing spiritual formation drop down where you can reach it, whole and complete.

Our culture, however, tends to train us in this manner. You do the right thing, put the money in the proper slot, push the right button and get the product you want at the bottom. Remember the vending machine where people do not get the product instantly? They start kicking and pounding on the machine. We have a tendency to do the same thing with God. We adopt some new spiritual technique. We find a new coin and a new slot to put it in. We put it in and push a new button, but nothing seems to happen. What do we do? We start kicking and beating on God: "Why don't you do something?" Or we discard that technique and go to find another machine and another coin.

The idea of spiritual growth as a continuous process rubs harshly against the deeply ingrained instant-gratification mode of our culture. Perhaps one of our first spiritual struggles for genuine growth toward wholeness will be against this strongly entrenched approach to life. There is much in our culture that infiltrates our attitudes unconsciously and makes us expect spiritual formation to happen instantaneously rather than through the steady progress of a process.

Option or Necessity?

Once we begin to realize that genuine spiritual growth is a continuous and sometimes difficult process, we may be tempted to think that it is an option we can take or leave. For many Christians, the quest for the deeper life in Christ is viewed as a discipline for the dedicated disciple, a pursuit for the particularly pious, a spiritual frill for those who have the time or inclination, a spiritual fad for trendy Christians.

We fail to realize that the process of spiritual shaping is a primal reality of human existence. *Everyone* is in a process of spiritual formation! Every thought we hold, every decision we make, every action we take, every emotion we allow to shape our behavior, every response we make to the world around us, every relationship we enter into, every reaction we have toward the things that surround us and impinge upon our lives—all of these things, little by little, are shaping us into some kind of being. We are being shaped into either the wholeness of the image of Christ or a horribly destructive caricature of that image—destructive not only to ourselves but also to others, for we inflict our brokenness upon them. This wholeness or destructiveness radically conditions our relationship with God, ourselves and others, as well as our involvement in the dehumanizing structures and dynamics of the broken world around us. We become either agents of God's healing and liberating grace or carriers of the sickness of the world. The direction of our spiritual growth infuses all we do with intimations of either Life or Death.

C. S. Lewis states it in his inimitable way:

Every time you make a choice you are turning the central part of you, the part of you that chooses, into something a little different from what it was before. And taking your life as a whole, with all your innumerable choices, all your life long you are slowly turning this central thing either into a heavenly creature or into a hellish creature: either into a creature that is in harmony with God, and with other creatures, and with itself, or else into one that is in a state of war and hatred with God, and with its fellow-creatures, and with itself. To be the one kind of creature is heaven: that is, it is joy and peace and knowledge and power. To be the other means madness, horror, idiocy, rage, impotence, and eternal loneliness. Each of us at each moment is progressing to the one state or the other.[4]

Spiritual formation is not an option! The inescapable conclusion is that life itself is a process of spiritual development. The only choice we have is whether that growth moves us toward wholeness in Christ or toward an increasingly dehumanized and destructive mode of being.

The Christian journey, therefore, is an intentional and continual commitment to a lifelong process of growth toward wholeness in Christ. It is a process of "growing up in every way into him who is the head, into Christ" (Eph 4:15), until we "attain to . . . mature personhood, to the measure of the stature of the fullness of Christ" (Eph 4:13). It is for this purpose that God is present and active in every moment of our lives.

Chapter 2

Being Conformed

*God of our creation and re-creation, you who are constantly at
work to shape me in the wholeness of Christ, you know the
hardness of the structures of my being that resist your shaping
touch. You know the deep inner rigidities of my being that reject
your changing grace. By your grace soften my hardness and rigid-
ity; help me to become pliable in your hands. Even as I read this,
may there be a melting of my innate resistance to your
transforming love.*

Spiritual formation is a process of *being conformed* to the image of
Christ, a journey into becoming persons of compassion, persons
who forgive, persons who care deeply for others and the world,
persons who offer themselves to God to become agents of divine
grace in the lives of others and their world—in brief, persons who
love and serve as Jesus did.

Now, if I had said spiritual formation was a process of "conforming ourselves" to the image of Christ, I suspect we would have been
much more comfortable. The difference between conforming ourselves and being conformed is the vital issue of *control*.

Almost from the moment of birth we engage in a struggle for
control of that portion of the world in which we live. Can we get
our parents to provide for our needs and wants when we want and

how we want? Can we get our playmates to play our way, or will they control us to play their way? Can we control situations and others to fulfill our agenda, or are we manipulated into serving others? Can we create enough of a security structure around our lives that we will be able to control life's adversities? Or, to put it in very contemporary terms, why shouldn't a woman's control of her life allow her to terminate the life of her unborn child? Why shouldn't my control of my life allow me to choose the time and means of its end? Why shouldn't we provide free contraceptives to our youth, so that their sexual behavior can be under their control and not under the control of the fear of sexually transmitted diseases? If you do not believe that control is a major issue in your life, study the ways you respond when someone or something disrupts your plan for the day.

Our constant struggle with the issue of control is a crucial part of our spiritual pilgrimage. I don't mind spiritual formation at all as long as I can be in control of it. As long as I can set the limits on its pace and its direction, I have no problem. What I do have a problem with is getting my control structures out of the way of my spiritual formation and letting God take control. In the final analysis, there is nothing we can do to transform ourselves into persons who love and serve as Jesus did except make ourselves available for God to do that work of transforming grace in our lives.

I'd Rather Do It Myself

This aspect of spiritual formation runs against the grain of our whole acculturation. We are a do-it-yourself culture. We are what I call an objectivizing, informational-functional culture.

An objectivizing culture is one that views the world primarily as an object "out there" to be grasped and controlled for our own purposes. We are the subjects whose role in life is to appropriate the objects in our world and use them to impose our will upon the world. The Quaker writer Parker Palmer describes it well:

We are well-educated people who have been schooled in a way of knowing that treats the world as an object to be dissected and manipulated, a way of knowing that gives us power over the world. . . . [We] have used [our] knowledge to rearrange the world to satisfy [our] drive for power, distorting and deranging life rather than loving it for the gift it is.[1]

"Being conformed" goes totally, radically against the ingrained objectification perspective of our culture. Graspers powerfully resist being grasped by God. Manipulators strongly reject being shaped by God. Controllers are inherently incapable of yielding control to God. Spiritual formation is the great reversal: from being the subject who controls all other things to being a person who is shaped by the presence, purpose and power of God in all things.

We are also an informational-functional culture. We seek to possess information, whether in the form of knowledge or in the form of techniques, in order that we might function more effectively to bring about the results we desire in the circumstances of our lives. We seek to be totally and completely in control of that process.

But there is an even deeper dimension of this need to control. We tend to see such control as essential to the meaning, value and purpose of our being. How much of the compulsive workaholism of our activities serves to authenticate ourselves as persons (to ourselves and others) and to prove that we have value, meaning and purpose in the world! To put it simply, we live as though our doing determined our being.

Jesus' Temptation—and Ours

Have you ever pondered the first temptation of Jesus (Mt 4:1-4)? Begin with the baptism where the heavens are opened, the Spirit comes down like a dove to rest upon Jesus, and a voice from heaven says, "This is my beloved Son, in whom I am well pleased" (Mt 3:16-17). The presence of the Spirit can be seen as Jesus' empowerment for ministry and "This is my Son" as Jesus' call to ministry.

Isn't it interesting that the Spirit, the source of Jesus' empowerment, is also focal in the temptation that follows—"The Spirit led
him into the wilderness to be tempted" (Mt 4:1)? We tend to think
of temptation as something totally alien to us, something from
"outside" that intrudes into our lives. We learn from Jesus' experience, however, that the most critical temptations attach themselves
to the call and empowerment of God that defines the meaning,
value and purpose of our existence. It was so for Jesus. His first
temptation went to the heart of who he was, and it is the temptation to which our culture has succumbed.

"*If* you are the Son of God, speak, that these stones may become
bread" (Mt 4:3). Do you see the nature of this temptation? The
temptation is for Jesus to use his empowerment by the Spirit to do
something that will authenticate God's call. More significantly, it is
a temptation to reverse the roles of being and doing, the temptation
to which our culture has succumbed. We tend to evaluate our own
meaning, value and purpose, as well as those of others, not by the
quality of our being but by what we do and how effectively we do
it.

I have a little game I play when traveling in airplanes and airports.
I regularly hear strangers meeting strangers, and usually within
thirty seconds to a minute one asks the other, "What do you do?"
Well, when someone asks me that question, I respond, "I teach in
a graduate school." Invariably I can see by their response, their body
language, that my "doing" places me in a fairly high category in
their value structure.

Of course their next question is either "What do you teach?" or
"Where do you teach?" When I say "New Testament" or "A theological seminary," in most cases I can see from their reaction that
they immediately and radically reverse their evaluation. From a
relatively high place in their ranking system I am quickly demoted
to one of the lower echelons.

Every time this has happened, the person has not even known my name. I have been categorized, labeled, cubbyholed and put away in their system of values simply by virtue of what I do.

We see some of the horribly destructive dynamics of this perspective in our culture at two extremes. For a long time, we have all been aware of the tremendously high suicide rate among young people up to about the age of twenty-five. I had suspected that, if the truth were known, we would discover that there was an equally high suicide rate among retired senior citizens. Then, in the spring of 1987, *Time* magazine published a cover article on suicide that showed some amazing statistics. The suicide rate among senior citizens was *double* the rate for adolescents! Later in the same year, *Modern Maturity* reported data from the National Center for Health Statistics that confirmed the *Time* article.[2]

Why is this so? Of course there is a complex mix of reasons for any suicide. I am not suggesting this as the sole reason for the problem, but I believe one of the underlying realities behind the epidemic of suicide among adolescents and senior citizens is that we are a culture that values people primarily for what they do. In our culture, persons' value, meaning and purpose reside primarily in the nature of their work. Teenagers don't "do" anything. Slinging hamburgers or bagging groceries isn't "doing" anything—not in the culture's value system. Adolescents are struggling to find their identity, struggling to find their personhood, struggling to find their personal integrity, struggling to find who they are in a culture that says you are what you do, but they are not ready to do much of anything yet.

And what happens to the person who wakes up one morning with a gold watch and a plaque expressing gratitude for forty years of service to the company—and nothing to do? All who have worked with the newly retired have seen them experience the despair and despondency of suddenly having to wrestle with the reality that what has given their whole life meaning, value, identity and purpose is no longer there. They don't know who they are anymore. For forty-five to fifty years they have "been" what they "did," and now they don't "do" anything anymore. Here we see some of the destructive dynamics of a perceptual framework that identifies our value, meaning, purpose and identity by what we do.

We live in a culture that has reversed the biblical order of being and doing. Being and doing are integrally related, to be sure, but we have to have the order straight. *Our doing flows out of our being.* In spiritual formation, the problem with being conformed is that we have a strong tendency to think that if only we *do* the right things we will *be* the right kind of Christian, as though our doing would bring about our being.

We will discuss this more fully in the section on spiritual disciplines, because there is, indeed, an interrelationship between our doing and God's acting. But we must always realize that it is God, not we ourselves, who is the source of the transformation of our being into wholeness in the image of Christ. Our part is to offer ourselves to God in ways that enable God to do that transforming work of grace. This is inherent in Jesus' response to his temptation, "People do not live by bread alone, but by every word that proceeds from the mouth of God" (Mt 4:4). Our relationship with God, not our doing, is the source of our being.

The Great Reversal

"Being conformed" militates against our very mode of being and way of life. Information graspers are structurally closed to being addressed by God. Information takers have extreme difficulty becoming receivers of God's voice. Functionally oriented people have great problems getting still and letting God act in God's own time. Performance-oriented persons have a powerful temptation to turn spiritual disciplines into "works righteousness."

Spiritual formation is the great reversal: from acting to bring about the desired results in our lives to being acted upon by God and responding in ways that allow God to bring about God's purposes. So to "lose one's self" in this context is to give up the deep inner informational-functional orientation that governs the lifestyle of our culture.

The restoration of being and doing to their proper relationship brings deadly consequences to the instant-gratification drive we considered in the description of spiritual formation as a process. When we operate from the perspective that our doing determines our being, we expect immediate returns on our investment of time and resources—observable results that prove that we have performed well and are therefore persons of value and worth. If we fail to receive such instant feedback, we presume we have failed and begin to struggle with a perceived loss of self-image, value, purpose and even identity. Instant-gratification persons have great difficulty waiting patiently for God's timing; trusting God to bring the needed transformation in God's time, not theirs; persevering in obedience even when there is no indication that such obedience is making any difference in their lives. "Being conformed" militates against our need for instant gratification.

Spiritual formation is the great reversal: from habitual expectation of closure to patient, open-ended yieldedness. To "lose one's self" in this context is to relinquish our self-generated expectations and desires for closure.

At the end of the Sermon on the Mount, Jesus deals with the interplay of being and doing in a rather frightening statement. He says, "Not everyone who says to me, 'Lord, Lord' shall enter the kingdom of heaven, but the one who does the will of my Father who is in heaven" (Mt 7:21). He seems to put all the emphasis upon doing, on the functional dynamics. But then Jesus continues, "On that day many will say to me, 'Lord, Lord, did we not prophesy in your name, and cast out demons in your name, and do many mighty works in your name?' " (Mt 7:22). Certainly these are the works of God, are they not—prophesying, casting out demons, doing many mighty works, all in Jesus' name?

Jesus doesn't contradict them. He does not say, "No, you didn't." He says, "I never knew you. Depart from me, you evildoers" (Mt 7:23). They had the works, the "doing," but they didn't have a relationship with Jesus, the "being," as the foundational reality out of which those works would flow. Jesus was pointing to the interrelationship between our doing and our being, but indicating that the order is from being to doing. The doing is an outflow, the result, of a being that exists in relationship with Jesus as Lord. So spiritual formation is not something that we do to ourselves or for ourselves, but something we allow God to do in us and for us as we yield ourselves to the work of God's transforming grace.

Thus, spiritual formation as "being conformed" brings its own spiritual work into our objectivizing, informational-functional, instant-gratification modes of being and doing. The first work of transformation is the reversal of these deeply ingrained and powerfully controlling dynamics of our cultural shaping. This means that our spiritual journey is not our setting out (by gathering information and applying it correctly) to find God (as an object "out there" to be grasped and controlled by us). It is a journey of learning to yield ourselves to God and discovering where God will take us.

Chapter 3

The Image of Christ

Gracious and loving God, it is with thankfulness that I hear your call to become Christlike. Something deep within my heart stirs in its heavy sleep at your call. The memory of something I was to have been, but am not, yet could still be flits on the fringes of my consciousness. O loving God, stir up this hunger in my heart until it becomes the all-consuming passion of my life.

---

*T*he process of spiritual formation is to conform us to *the image of Christ*. When the New Testament writers speak of "the image of Christ," they mean the fulfillment of the deepest dynamics of our being. We are created to be compassionate persons whose relationships are characterized by love and forgiveness, persons whose lives are a healing, liberating, transforming touch of God's grace upon their world. When all of us are perfectly conformed to the image of Christ, we will not be a group of clones. In fact, we find our unique individuality only to the extent that we are fully conformed to the image of Christ.

Have you ever noticed how the world wants to squeeze us all into the same mold? It is the world's perspective that wants to clone us so that we will all use the same toothpaste, mouthwash, hair spray and deodorant; wear the same clothes; eat the same food; drive the same cars; and generally fulfill Madison Avenue's image of success. It is only in Christ that we find our individuality. We become compassionate persons in an infinite variety of models. We love and serve like Jesus in unique ways.

Added On or Built In?

Often people have the idea that the image of Christ is something alien to human beings, something strange that God wants to add on to our life, something imposed upon us from outside that doesn't really fit us. In reality, however, the image of Christ is the fulfillment of the deepest hungers of the human heart for wholeness. The greatest thirst of our being is for fulfillment in Christ's image. The most profound yearning of the human spirit, which we try to fill with all sorts of inadequate substitutes, is the yearning for our completeness in the image of Christ.

The image of Christ is that which brings cleansing, healing, restoration, renewal, transformation and wholeness into the unclean, diseased, broken, imprisoned, dead incompleteness of our lives. It brings compassion in place of indifference, forgiveness in place of resentment, kindness in place of coldness, openness in place of protective defensiveness or manipulation, a life lived for God and not self. Again and again the New Testament emphasizes that this is the work God is seeking to do in us—to grow us up into Christlikeness: "We all with unveiled face, beholding the glory of the Lord, are being changed into his likeness" (2 Cor 3:18) "until we all attain . . . to mature personhood, to the measure of the stature of the fullness of Christ" (Eph 4:13), "seeing that we have put off the old nature with its practices and have put on the new nature, which is being renewed in knowledge after the image of its Creator" (Col 3:9-10).

Paul probes the profound depths of our relationship to the image of Christ in Ephesians 1:3-6:

Blessed the God and Father of our Lord Jesus Christ, who has blessed us in Christ with every spiritual blessing in the heavenly places, just as he chose us in Christ before the foundation of the world to be holy and blameless before him in love. He destined us for adoption as his children through Jesus Christ, according to the good pleasure of his will, to the praise of his glorious grace, which he freely bestowed on us in the Beloved.

This is a profound and powerful affirmation of the nature of our being. Its focus is found in the affirmation that God "chose us in Christ before the foundation of the world to be holy and blameless before him in love." The word *chose* translates a compound Greek term which literally means "spoke forth." Paul is not saying that God chooses some and does not choose others. Paul is saying that every human being has been "spoken forth" by God *before the foundation of the world*. Paul is alluding to the account in Genesis where God speaks forth creation into being. He is indicating that there was no surprise in heaven when any of us were conceived. There may have been a surprise in our mother's or father's life, but there was no surprise in heaven. God purposed us into being before the foundation of the world. This is a powerfully liberating word for persons whose conception was an "accident" and whose birth was unwanted.

I once heard a woman tell of her struggle with this reality. Her mother was a prostitute, and she was the accidental byproduct of her mother's occupation. Although her life's pilgrimage had brought her to faith in Christ, blessed her with a deeply Christian husband and beautiful children, and given her a life of love and stability, she was obsessed with the need to find out who her father was. This obsession was affecting her marriage, her family and her life.

She told how one day she was standing at the kitchen sink, washing the dishes, with tears of anguish and frustration running down her face into the dishwater. In her agony, she cried out, "Oh, God, *who* is my father?" Then, she said, she heard a voice saying to her, "I am your father."

The voice was so real she turned to see who had come into the kitchen, but there was no one there. Again the voice came, "I am your father, and I have always been your father."

In that moment she knew the profound reality of which Paul is speaking. She came to know that deeper than the "accident" of her conception was the eternal purpose of a loving God, who had spoken her forth into being before the foundation of the world.

But Paul indicates that God didn't just purpose us into being. God purposes us into a particular kind of being—that we might be holy and blameless before God in love. We were created to be whole (holy) in the nature of our being and to be persons of complete integrity (blameless) in our doing. In fact, we are to find the fulfillment of our being in being like Christ. This is why Paul says that God spoke us forth *in Christ*. To facilitate this wholeness of life, God "blessed us *in Christ* with every spiritual blessing in the heavenly places." Our life, in all its particularity, is encompassed about in all its details with every spiritual blessing of God's order of wholeness and life.

Points of Unlikeness

Only a moment's reflection will reveal that something has gone wrong with God's plan for our wholeness. Although we have been spoken forth by God to be whole persons in the image of Christ and supplied with every resource necessary for the fulfillment of that objective, we have failed to achieve God's purposes for us. This is why Paul adds, "He destined us for adoption as his children through Jesus Christ, according to the good pleasure of his will, to the praise of his glorious grace, which he freely bestowed on us in the Beloved." Even in our failure and incompleteness, in the brokenness and bondage that hinder our growth toward wholeness in Christ, it is still the good pleasure of God's will that we should become God's children.

The process of being conformed to the image of Christ takes place primarily at the points of our unlikeness to Christ's image. God is present to us in the most destructive aspects of our cultural captivity. God is involved with us in the most imprisoning bondage of our brokenness. God meets us in those places of our lives that are most alienated from God. God is there, in grace, offering us the forgiveness, the cleansing, the liberation, the healing we need to begin the journey toward our wholeness and fulfillment in Christ.

But this can be uncomfortable. We would much rather have our spiritual formation focus on those places where we are pretty well along the way. How much of our devotional life and our worship are designed simply to affirm, for ourselves, others and perhaps even God, those areas of our lives that we think are already well along the way. In fact, may not such practices become a defense mechanism against the areas that are not yet conformed to the image of Christ?

If, indeed, the work of God's formation in us is the process of conforming us to the image of Christ, obviously it's going to take place at the points where we are not yet conformed to that image. This means that one of the first dynamics of holistic spiritual formation will be confrontation. Through some channel—the Scripture, worship, a word of proclamation, the agency of a brother or sister in Christ, even the agency of an unbeliever—the Spirit of God may probe some area in which we are not conformed to the image of Christ. That probing will probably always be confrontational, and it will always be a challenge and a call to us in our brokenness to come out of the brokenness into wholeness in Christ. But it will also be a costly call, because that brokenness is who we are.

Sometimes we suffer under the illusion that our incompleteness, our brokenness, our deadness is something like a sweater that we can easily unbutton and slip off. It is not that easy. Our brokenness *is* us. Like Pogo, "we have met the enemy and he is us." This is what

Jesus indicates when he speaks about losing yourself. That in you which has not yet been conformed to the image of Christ is not simply a "thing" in you—it is an essential part of who you are. This is what Jesus is pointing to when he calls us to take up our cross.

Our cross is not that cantankerous person we have to deal with day by day. Our cross is not the employer we just can't get along with. Our cross is not that neighbor or work colleague who cuts across the grain in every single time of relationship. Nor is our cross the difficulties and infirmities that the flow of life brings to us beyond our control. Our cross is the point of our unlikeness to the image of Christ, where we must die to self in order to be raised by God into wholeness of life in the image of Christ *right there at that point.* So the process of being conformed to the image of Christ takes place at the points of our unlikeness to Christ, and the first step is confrontation.

The second dynamic in holistic spiritual formation is consecration. We must come to the point of saying yes to God at each point of unlikeness. We must give God permission to do the work God wants to do with us right there, because transformation will not be forced upon us. God will stand at those closed doors of our lives by which we have shut God out and imprisoned ourselves within, and the love of God's grace will knock and knock and knock with the knock of confrontation upon those doors, but God will not force open the doors. As George MacDonald says, "He watches to see the door move from within."[1] There must be a consecration, a release of ourselves to God at each point of our unlikeness to Christ. When there is, the process of being conformed to the image of Christ begins.

In part three, "The Journey," when we discuss spiritual disciplines, we will see how that release takes place. Spiritual disciplines are the act of releasing ourselves in a consistent manner to God, opening those doors in a regular way to allow God's transforming work in our lives. When we respond to the confrontation of the

Spirit at the point of our brokenness with a consecration that allows God to do the work God wants to do, we begin to experience the reality of being conformed to the image of Christ.

There are times, I grant you, when the nature of our response is such that God, you might think, would instantly touch us into wholeness. But I have discovered in my own life and in reading the saints of the church that those times are the exceptions. The rule is that God begins to work with us there and to grow us up into wholeness over a period of time as we continue to offer the disciplines as a means of grace.

Chapter 4

For the Sake
of Others

*Gracious God, from whom every family in heaven and on earth is
named, deliver me, I pray, from the easy habit of thinking that my
spirituality is something between you and me alone. It is so
difficult to accept the idea that my spiritual wholeness cannot be
attained outside of my life with others. Help me to open my heart
and spirit to what you want to say to me in this chapter. Help me
to commit my relationships to you, that they may become channels
of your grace in my life and that I may become a channel of your
grace for others.*

---

*T*he fourth element in our definition of spiritual formation, *for the
sake of others*, is the one we must never forget. Everything that God
has done, is doing and ever will do in our lives to conform us to the
image of Christ (which is the image of our wholeness) is not so that
we may someday be set in a display case in heaven as trophies of
grace. All of God's work to conform us to the image of Christ has
as its sole purpose that we might become what God created us to
be *in relationship with God and with others*. This is why Jesus summarized
the whole law in the command to "love the Lord your God with all

your heart, and with all your soul, and with all your mind, and with all your strength" and "love your neighbor as yourself" (Mk 12:30-31), and why the New Testament writers regularly lift up love for neighbor as the essence of the Christian life (Rom 13:9-10; 1 Cor 13; Gal 5:14; Eph 4:15-16; 5:2; Col 3:14; 1 Thess 4:9-10; Jas 2:8; 1 Pet 1:22; 4:8; 1 Jn 3:10-14, 17-18, 23; 4:7-8, 11-12, 19-21—to note a few).

Being like Christ

If there is any truth in the rest of our definition, particularly the aspect of being conformed to the image of Christ, reflect for a moment on what the image of Christ is. It is the image of One who gave himself totally, completely, absolutely, unconditionally for others. This is the direction in which the Spirit of God moves us toward wholeness. If we forget this, if we short-circuit our definition (as many definitions do at this point), we don't have Christian spiritual formation, we don't have holistic spiritual formation. What we have is some kind of pathological formation that is very privatized and individualized, a spiritualized form of self-actualization. Although such forms of spirituality may be very appealing to look at on the outside, quite comfortable in their easy conformity to the values and dynamics of our culture, they are like a whitewashed tomb that has deadness on the inside if they are not life-giving, healing and redemptive *for others.*

Wherever there is something in our life that is not conformed to the image of Christ, there is a place where we are incapable of being all that God wants us to be with others; there is a place where our life with others is hindered and limited and restricted in its effectiveness and in its fullness; there is a place where our life will tend to become disruptive and even destructive to others. We can never be all that God wants us to be with others as long as that point of unlikeness to the image of Christ exists within us.

You see, the points of our unlikeness to Christ are areas of our life where we are lord and not Christ—areas where our agenda, our will, our desire, our purposes rule. Wherever this is the case, our relationship with others will be controlled not by God's will but by our own agenda. Our relationship with others at that point will become manipulative as we attempt to impose our agenda on them. If others do not readily succumb to our manipulations, we will tend to become abusive with them or break the relationship entirely.

Testing Our Spiritual Growth

If you want a good litmus test of your spiritual growth, simply examine the nature and quality of your relationships with others. Are you more loving, more compassionate, more patient, more understanding, more caring, more giving, more forgiving than you were a year ago? If you cannot answer these kinds of questions in the affirmative and, especially, if others cannot answer them in the affirmative about you, then you need to examine carefully the nature of your spiritual life and growth.

As we noted above, Jesus inseparably joined loving God with loving others, and John reminds us that "the one who claims to be in the light and hates others is in the darkness still. The one who loves others abides in the light and is not a cause of stumbling. But the one who hates others is in the darkness and walks in the darkness, and does not know the way, because the darkness brings blindness of outlook" (1 Jn 2:9-10). Paul puts it in a different frame of reference when he writes to congregations of (1) their faith in the Lord Jesus and (2) the love they have for others (Gal 5:6; Eph 1:15; Col 1:4; 1 Thess 1:3; 3:6; 5:8; 2 Tim 1:13; Philem 4-5), and especially when he links growth in faith with increasing love for others: "Your faith is growing abundantly, and the love of every one of you for one another is increasing" (2 Thess 1:3).

Our relationships with others are not only the testing grounds of our spiritual life but also the places where our growth toward wholeness in Christ happens. There is a temptation to think that our spiritual growth takes place in the privacy of our personal relationship with God and then, once it is sufficiently developed, we can export it into our relationships with others and "be Christian" with them. But holistic spirituality, the process of being conformed to the image of Christ, takes place in the midst of our relationships with others, not apart from them. We learn to be Christ's for others by seeking to be yielded and obedient to God in the midst of our relationships.

We will examine this more fully in the final section of this book, "Companions on the Way: Corporate and Social Spirituality." At this point we only need to be sensitive to the fact that for most people spiritual life and growth toward wholeness in Christ have their focus in God and self. A focus on others is rarely at the same level. Relationships with others are often seen as secondary and tangential to the primary relationship with God. Holistic spiritual growth moves against that grain. The primary focus must be trinitarian—God, self, others—if we are to grow holistically into the image of Christ. Every relationship has the potential of becoming the place of transforming encounter with God, and every advance in the spiritual life has its necessary and immediate corollary in the transformation of our relationships with others.

The emphasis upon spiritual formation for the sake of others can be seen in the story of the Rescue Society. Along a reef-ridden, rockbound coast, a small group became concerned about those who were losing their lives in the shipwrecks that took place on the reefs and rocks. They formed the Rescue Society for the purpose of saving those who had been shipwrecked. For years they risked themselves to save others, often losing their own lives for the sake of others, but hundreds were saved who otherwise would have been lost.

As a new generation entered the Rescue Society, they decided to perfect their techniques for rescue so that even more could be saved. They began to attend rescue workshops, to bring in consultants on the latest rescue techniques, to entertain salespeople who touted the latest in rescue equipment. Before long, the maintenance and perfection of the rescue station, its techniques, its equipment, became the focus of the Rescue Society.

One night, while the entire Rescue Society was attending yet another meeting to perfect their rescue skills, a great passenger liner struck upon the reef and sank. Hundreds of people were lost because there was no one left to go to their rescue. The Rescue Society had come to exist for its own perfection and not for the sake of others.

Part II
The Vehicle:
Personality
and Piety

I n this section we will explore the value of Carl Jung's model of
human personality for holistic spirituality and examine the insights developmental psychology can bring to our spiritual pilgrimage. To use Jung for this purpose is not to endorse the totality
of either his psychological construct or his worldview, but simply
to recognize that some of his observations about human existence
can be instructive for our spiritual pilgrimage.

First (chapter five), we will consider an overview of the Jungian
model of personality types, with an emphasis on the dynamic and
ever-modulating aspects of our being and doing. We will look at the
role of our preferred ways of being and doing in the world: how we
prefer either extraversion or introversion as our focus of life, sensing or intuition as our means of receiving data for living, thinking
or feeling as our way of processing the data, and perception or
judging as our way of relating to the world. We will also consider

the need for a balanced integration of our preferred ways with our less preferred ways of being and doing for holistic spirituality. We will see that spiritual and psychological wholeness calls for a balanced interplay between our preferred and less preferred ways of being and doing.

With this backdrop in place, we will then examine spiritual formation (chapter six). We will look at our strongly ingrained tendency to adopt patterns of spirituality which favor our preferences but which, if not balanced with spiritual disciplines that nurture our less preferred ways of being and doing, can become destructive of spiritual wholeness. We will see that holistic spirituality nurtures our whole person and not simply our preferred ways of operating (chapter seven).

We need to realize that not only is psychology not a substitute for spirituality, but spirituality is not a substitute for psychology. While most Christians would not tend to make the first assertion, many would and do tend to make the second. As we have already noted, spiritual formation is often seen as the answer to all problems. Often profound, deep-seated psychological problems are met with demands for deeper faith, more rigorous obedience, more vital spirituality. Psychological brokenness needs treatment in the same way that a broken bone needs to be set and healed. While physical therapy is an integral and essential aspect of healing for a broken leg, the therapy alone, without setting of the bone, will never enable the bone to heal properly. Likewise, spiritual formation is an integral and essential part of recovery of human wholeness from psychological brokenness, but spiritual formation alone will never bring full and complete wholeness of being.

There may come points in our spiritual pilgrimage when the Spirit of God awakens us to some area of deep psychological imbalance or brokenness within. At those points, sound psychological therapy becomes an essential component of our spiritual journey. Psychological therapy, carried out within a Christian understanding of human nature, can richly enhance spiritual formation, just as holistic spiritual formation always enhances sound psychological treatment. Neither of these is a substitute for the other, but they work together as means of grace through which God conforms us to the image of Christ for the sake of others.

Chapter 5
Creation Gifts

Thank you, O God, for meeting me here in ways far beyond my knowing. I thank you for working in me in ways far deeper than my awareness. I thank you for your love. It enfolds me even when I am most resistant to your presence. I thank you for your grace. It offers yourself to me even when my back is turned. I thank you, as I come into your presence in this chapter, for the infinite variety of your creative power in my life. I thank you for the infinite diversity that you have crafted into me. It makes me a unique person. As I think upon this, I pray that you will enable me to be truly thankful for the creation gifts you have given me. Enable me to offer myself to you in them for the work you want to do in me and through me in my life in the world.

---

*P*aul wrote to the factionalized Christians in Corinth:

For just as the body is one and has many members, and all the members of the body, though many, are one body, so it is with Christ. For by one Spirit we were all baptized into one body—Jews or Greeks, slaves or free—and all were made to drink of one Spirit. For the body does not consist of one member but of many. (1 Cor 12:12-14)

In this passage, and the illustration that follows in the text, Paul puts his finger on an issue of crucial significance to holistic spirituality. Paul implies that our spiritual journey, while it is unique to each of us as an individual member of the body of Christ, is not an isolated pilgrimage but is part of a sort of caravan with the diverse members of the body. Paul touches here upon the vital issue of the relationship between the individual and the faith community, especially the relationship of the uniqueness of individual persons to the community and the community to them.

With his metaphor of the body in 1 Corinthians 12, Paul emphasizes both the vital reality of the community of faith as a living organism (it is a body, even the body of Christ) and the uniqueness of each individual member of that community. The faith community is not a homogeneous collection of individuals among whom there is no distinction. Nor are the individuals in the community of faith isolated, independent entities without any essential reference to one another. Paul's emphasis is on the *interdependence* of the individual members of the community of faith.

There is no holistic spirituality for the individual outside of the community of faith. In fact, to use Paul's image, the holistic spirituality of the individual is essential for the spiritual health of the community, and the health of the community is essential for the spiritual wholeness of the individual. Just as each cell in our physical body depends upon the body for its life and the well-being of the body depends upon the wholeness of each individual cell, the individual Christian can be whole only through interdependent interaction with the other members of the faith community.

This reality provides the deeper context in which we consider our unique *creation gifts*,[1] those very personal and individual structures of our personality preferences that characterize our being and doing. These unique creation gifts are God's means of grace for the enrichment of our community of faith, and our community of faith is the means of grace by which God nurtures the fullness of our creation gifts.

Our Creation Gifts
Jungian psychology provides us with a helpful model to illustrate

one aspect of how our mutual interdependence enriches and enhances our growth toward wholeness in Christ. Over the years of his study of human behavior, Carl Jung discovered that human beings have four essential preferences that shape the way they relate to the world around them and process the data they receive from that world. Jung organized these preferences in four pairs. The four basic pairs of preference are extraversion (E) and introversion (I), sensing (S) and intuition (N), thinking (T) and feeling (F), judgment (J) and perception (P). Within each pair, persons generally prefer one mode of behavior over the other; one behavior is preferred, the other is less preferred.

The first pair of preferences relate to where persons find their preferred focus—whether in the outer world of persons, events and things (E) or in the inner world of self and ideas (I). Extraverts tend to be "people persons." They enjoy the company of others and are energized by fellowship with others. They are good at remembering names. They like to be actively engaged with others in work and play. Introverts, while certainly not people-haters, tend to prefer solitude to fellowship. They have difficulty remembering names. They prefer to work and play by themselves and tend toward reflection rather than action. At social gatherings, extraverts will be found actively mingling about, interacting with others, while the introverts tend to find a space on the edges and let the extraverts come to them.

The second pair of preferences, intuition and sensing, have to do with persons' preferred means of receiving information for their living—either through primary reliance upon intuition, the inner "urgings" of the spirit (N), or primarily through their physical senses (S). Intuitive persons are problem solvers. They enjoy envisioning a way to bring order to a complicated situation and then doing it. But then they move on to another problem. They do not like repetitive activity and can be impatient with details. Sensing persons like routine and details and enjoy established ways of doing things. They tend to be good with work that requires precision.

The third pair of preferences, thinking and feeling, suggest the means for processing the data received through intuition and sensing—either a primary reliance upon the cognitive processes of reasoning (T) or a primary reliance upon the stirrings of the heart (F). Thinking persons do not show emotion easily and tend to be uncomfortable around those who do. They are very analytical and logical and tend to make decisions in an impersonal way, sometimes hurting others without being aware of it. Whatever disciple said, "What a waste! This ointment could have been sold and the money given to the poor" (Mt 26:8-9), was a thinking person. Feeling persons, however, are very sensitive to how others feel. They like harmony. They have a need to please others and sometimes let their decisions be influenced by others' likes or dislikes as well as by their own.

The final pair of preferences, judgment and perception, have to do with a person's preferred relationship to the flow of life—either a primary desire for closure and completion, order and control (J) or a primarily open-ended and laid-back approach to life (P).[2] I can always tell the J and P preference students in my classes. The J preference students usually have their work in on time or even early. The P preference students often come in just before the deadline and ask for an extension.

We all have both options of each pair available to us. These preferences are part of the equipment we are created with, what Reginald Johnson calls our "creation gifts." Our preferred modes of employing these gifts have been developed as we progressed through the stages of our psychological development.[3]

Our Individuality
In some persons, each of these preferences is very clearly delineated. In other persons, the alternatives in one or more of the pairs may be almost equally strong. Let us use extraversion/introversion as an illustration. Some persons have a very strong preference for

extraversion. They crave being with others, being active and involved in everything going on around them. Being with others revitalizes them; involvement in activities energizes them. Being alone, generally, is to be avoided at all costs. Other persons have an equally strong preference for introversion. They crave times of solitude and enjoy working alone on projects or activities. Unrelieved fellowship with others is debilitating. Solitude energizes them, invigorates them. In contrast to these strong preferences, however, some persons are equally comfortable with either preference and can move with relative ease from extraversion to introversion and back again.

One image for appreciating these differences in preference is "handedness." Some persons are left-handed, some right-handed, and some ambidextrous. Left-handed persons are not "correct" while right-handed persons are "incorrect." There is no "true" or "false" involved in this, nor in our preferred modes of being and doing in the world. Extraverts are not "right" and introverts "wrong." Neither is inherently better than the other. Our preferences simply delineate the basic structure of our approach to life.

According to Jung's model, persons fall into one of sixteen basic preference patterns:

INTJ	INTP	INFJ	INFP
ISTJ	ISTP	ISFJ	ISFP
ENTJ	ENTP	ENFJ	ENFP
ESTJ	ESTP	ESFJ	ESFP[4]

You are undoubtedly thinking that surely there are many more patterns than this. You yourself know more than sixteen different types of people. This is because there is the possibility of an almost infinite diversity within any given preference pattern. Among a group of INFPs, for instance, there can be a tremendous diversity in the strength of each pair of preferences. At one end of the spectrum will be INFP persons who have an extremely strong preference for introversion over extraversion; at the other end will be

INFPs whose preference for introversion is only minimally stronger than their preference for extraversion. Even if two INFP persons should have equally strong (or weak) preferences for introversion, their preferences for intuition (N) may then be at wide variance— one strongly preferring intuition over sensing, the other only barely preferring sensing less than intuition. The same also holds true for their preferences for feeling (F) over thinking and perception (P) over judgment. This means that each person within each one of the sixteen basic patterns remains a unique individual, distinct even from others of the same pattern of preferences.

In addition to the strengths of our preferences, a multitude of factors determine our differences from one another: birth order, family history, sociocultural upbringing, stages of development and so forth. These factors all interplay with our pattern of preferences and lead to the subtle and not so subtle shadings of our differences. Thus you can see that there is an infinite variety of possibilities, and this is part of the wonderful diversity with which God has created us.

A person's pattern of preference, however, should not be viewed as a straitjacket that locks him or her into predetermined modes of being and doing. The patterns indicate preferences, not rules of behavior. Human wholeness lies not in seeking to become an "XXXX," a person with no distinct preference in any of the pairs, but in a mature and discriminating ability to function with whichever side of the preference pair is best suited to the situation at hand. There are numerous times daily when each of us finds that we cannot simply exercise our preferred pattern. Those who prefer introversion find themselves required to function as extraverts if they are to be effective in a given situation. Those who prefer the thinking process find themselves called to lead with the heart if their contribution to the issue at hand is to be creative. Those who prefer the judgment mode of control and closure find it necessary to resist imposing control and to defer decision so that the ultimate closure can be a wholesome solution to the issue.

Our image of handedness can again help us here. Even though I am right-handed, I would be greatly disadvantaged should I lose the use of my left hand. There are times when my right hand needs the help of the left, and other times when the left must do the job itself. So it is with our preferences.

A Problem

One of the major problems of our lives is our tendency to evaluate our pattern of preference as being superior (or perhaps inferior) to the patterns of others. Here is where Paul (slightly adapted!) sensitizes us to one of the essential dimensions of our life together in the community of faith:

> For the community of faith does not consist of one pattern of preference but of many. If the INTJ should say, "Because I am not an ESFP, I do not belong to the community," that would not make it any less a part of the community. And if the INTP should say, "Because I am not an ESFJ, I do not belong to the community," that would not make it any less a part of the community. If the whole community were an INFJ, where would be the ESTP? If the whole community were an INFP, where would be the ESTJ?   The ISTJ cannot say to the ENFP, "I have no need of you," nor again the ISTP to the ENFJ, "I have no need of you." (1 Cor 12:14-21)

The problem for the Corinthians, and for us, is the tendency to view one's own pattern of preferences as the norm. We expect others to conform to our norm, to be like us, to approach life in our way. Alternatively (and usually pathologically), we think that we should be like others and relate to the world and respond to life as they do. Worse than either of these, however, is our tendency to view alternate patterns of preference as "unusual," perhaps "wrong," and then even "evil." When this happens, we are in serious trouble.

What about the other side of our own preference pattern? If a strong INTJ views a strong ESFP as an inherently "wrong" or "evil" person, what happens to the INTJ's relationship with the shadow side of his or her own being—the ESFP which is the other side of the INTJ preference? As you may suspect, at this point serious problems can arise related not only to our own psychological wholeness but also to our spiritual wholeness.

Chapter 6

One-Sided Spirituality

Thank you, gracious God, for your steadfast love and patience with me. Even though I persist in the misuse of the creation gifts you have given me, you continue to call me out of my incompleteness into the wholeness you have for me in Christ. Even when I try to hide behind a "spirituality" that confirms me in my incompleteness and brokenness, your love neither abandons me nor tolerates my evasions. Your love becomes troubling grace that shakes my foundations and breaches my defenses. Help me to let you do your disturbing work in my life in this chapter. Let it become for me a mirror in which you show me what you want me to see about myself.

---

*L*eft to ourselves in the development of our spiritual practices, we will generally gravitate to those spiritual activities that nurture our preferred pattern of being and doing. The shadow side of our preference pattern will languish unattended and unnurtured. For instance, extraverts will tend to develop a highly social spirituality which involves them in spiritual activities with others, but avoid the solitude and reflection that would bring depth and perspective to their life with others. Intuitive persons will tend to develop more contemplative forms of spirituality, but minimize the input of their senses that would help to keep their vision and intuition in touch with "reality." Thinking persons will tend to be more "theological," more analytical and structural in their spirituality. Theory and principles of spiritual life will be their focus, but they may slight the affective, emotional aspects of their relationship with God and others that could keep their spirituality from becoming a legalism. Perception-oriented persons will tend to lean toward a very unplanned, unstructured spirituality that is open to God in whatever comes, but resist a more planned and structured spirituality that would bring some order and regularity to their spontaneity.

The results of such one-sided spirituality can be devastating to our spiritual pilgrimage. The undernourished shadow side will, sooner or later, demand equal time. Not having any holistic spiritual patterns for its expression, it will usually manifest itself in "unspiritual" behaviors which are both antithetical to holistic spirituality and destructive to the spiritual activities of our preferred patterns. For example, in the next chapter we will see that one of the special temptations for intuitive-type persons is primitive sensuality. Why? Because if their sensing side is not nurtured spiritually, it may fulfill its needs through sensual activities that are destructive. One wonders, for instance, how many of the sexual aberrations of noted Christian leaders in recent years might be due in part to their being strongly intuitive types who failed to nurture the sensing side of their preference pattern.

Or take the thinking-type persons whose special temptation is emotional explosion. Why? Because if they do not bring their feeling side into their spiritual life and deal with their feelings and emotions in a holistic way, those pent-up emotions will, sooner or later, "explode" in damaging ways. When this happens, it tends to "confirm" our mistaken idea that our shadow side is evil, and we redouble our efforts in the areas of our preferences in an attempt to overcome the "evil." Many people ride this spiritual rollercoaster throughout their Christian pilgrimage, because no one ever tells them that their shadow side needs equal time and attention in their spiritual activities.

There are spiritual activities that nurture each of our preferred modes of being and doing. If we are strong introvert-intuitive types, chances are we have developed a spirituality that is very privatized, reflective, contemplative and individualized. Introvert-intuitive types will seek to spend time in monastic settings if these are available. This can be a real spiritual high for them. But take extravert-sensing persons to a Cistercian monastery with its vows of silence, and they will "climb the walls." I saw it happen once. A group of us went on a weekend retreat to the Abbey of Gethsemani (where Thomas Merton lived). We went just before the beginning of the new academic year to be spiritually renewed, to reflect and to let God prepare us for the coming year. One fellow who came along was a very strong extravert-sensing-feeling person. We arrived Friday in time for the afternoon liturgy and stayed through Sunday afternoon, so we had a full forty-eight hours. By noon on Saturday, this poor fellow was practically a basket case. He was out walking in the gardens, through the woods, along the roads, up and down the halls, reading every book he could find in the library, trying to fill the long silent minutes with some stimulus. He was terribly disoriented and uncomfortable, because the monastic retreat was not a form of spirituality that nurtured his preference.

Spiritual Tendencies

Each of us will tend to develop models of spiritual life that nurture our preference pattern. If extraversion is our dominant preference, we are going to select models of spirituality that bring us together with other people in worship, fellowship groups, prayer groups, Bible-study groups, spiritual-formation groups. We will want corporate spirituality and will not get as much out of private, individualized spirituality. If our preference is introversion, we will adopt models of spirituality that emphasize solitude, reflection, meditation, contemplation. We will not get as much out of corporate experiences of spirituality as the extravert.

If sensing is our preferred mode, we will develop forms of spiritual activities which build upon the use of our senses. We will probably find incense a help in prayer, chanting psalms or hymns a means of communion with God and our inner being. Listening to inspiring music or the sounds of nature will lift us into the presence of God; working with paints or clay may be a means of worship; icons, symbols and the movement of liturgy will become visual means of grace. If, however, intuition is our preferred pattern, the creative use of our imagination, re-creating in our mind's eye the scenes of biblical passages, listening to the thoughts and ideas that emerge from within will characterize our spiritual patterns.

Should thinking be one of our preferences, we will tend to be cerebral in our spirituality. We will appreciate reason as the means through which we encounter God; we'll tend to be analytical and theoretical in our wrestling with the Scripture, preferring to theologize abstractly on an issue rather than struggle with its personal appropriation in our daily life. Should feeling be our preference, however, our spiritual habits will tend to focus more on relationships—with God and others. We will encounter God through our relationships and the emotions attendant upon them, our prayer will tend to be affective—emerging more often from our feelings than from our thoughts—and we will seek to incarnate our spiritual insights in our relationships with others.

Finally, if we have a strong preference for judgment, our spiritual life will probably be very highly structured and regulated. Devotional practices will be planned, usually following a well-developed pattern; reading of Scripture will be very systematic, and we will have a tendency to "control" our relationship with God. If, on the other hand, our preference is perception, we might find it difficult to develop a regular or structured set of spiritual practices. We will tend to take our spirituality where we find it or when there happens to be some time. We will appreciate spontaneity in both individual and corporate forms of spirituality and quickly become restless with regularity and ordered forms of worship.

While such preferred patterns of spirituality can be a powerful means of God's grace in our growth toward wholeness in Christ, the following story will illustrate the dangers involved in a one-sided spirituality. A student came to me a few years ago and, after breaking the ice, admitted to me somewhat sheepishly, "My devotional time is the pits. I'm just getting nothing out of it."

I asked, "What are you doing?"

He responded, "Well, I have a quiet place in the apartment where I go and I sit. I try to get silent, I read the Scripture, I pray, and I try to meditate. It's just horrible."

Since we have all our students take the Myers-Briggs Type Indicator[1] as part of their orientation, I inquired about his preference pattern. It turned out that he was an ESFP with strong sensing-feeling preferences. When I asked him how he had developed this kind of devotional life, he said, "I was taught that if you want to have a good devotional life you go aside by yourself and sit quietly, read your Bible, pray and try to be silent and meditate and listen to God."

I asked him, "What are some of the times God has truly been alive for you, when God's presence has been real?"

He replied, "When I am out walking in the woods and hearing the sounds of nature and things like that." And he went on to describe a pattern of sensing-feeling activities.

I suggested to him that perhaps he should develop a devotional time that would incorporate these kinds of activities. Since he had his devotions early in the morning, I suggested that he go out and walk through the streets of town or in the woods while he prayed, pondered Scripture and fellowshipped with God. When I discovered he had several records or tapes that contained only nature sounds—flowing water, birds, wind in the trees, ocean surf, whale songs and the like—I proposed that if for some reason he couldn't go out, he put one of these on and use it as the context for his devotional time. I also suggested that instead of sitting still he might try expressing his prayer and worship of God in body movements, singing hymns and chanting the psalms.

Although he didn't say it in words, I could see him wondering whether this was appropriate. Could these kinds of activities really be "devotions"? I tried to assure him they were.

A few weeks later the young man returned ecstatic. He had experienced a wonderful renewal of spiritual vitality and a sense of once again being on the pilgrimage toward wholeness in Christ.

What had happened? Some well-intentioned INTJ had laid upon this fellow, in the early stages of his Christian pilgrimage, a purely INTJ devotional life. Such a model of devotion can be rich and fulfilling for an INTJ, but not for an ESFP. It didn't nurture this kind of person at all. It had become a numbing burden rather than a nurturing blessing.

The Potential for Disintegration

For me, this was a powerful illustration of how we tend to develop spiritual activities that are conducive to our preference pattern and then think that this is the only viable pattern of spirituality for others. Yet there is a danger in this awareness. For in order to develop holistically in our spirituality, we also need to nurture our shadow side. One-sided spirituality, while it may be comfortable and may seem to be advancing us on our spiritual pilgrimage, will ultimately begin to disintegrate under pressures for nurture from our shadow side.

Such a disintegration takes two basic forms. The first is the disintegration of our spiritual pilgrimage itself. For some this will take the form of what John Wesley called the "shipwreck of faith." Such persons will fall away from the faith, their spiritual practices will wane and disappear, and finally they will abandon any pretense of Christian faith and practice. For others, the disintegration will take the form of stagnation. While they continue to participate in the life of the Christian community and maintain a set of spiritual practices, the result is a spiritual façade. They have a "form of godliness without the power" (2 Tim 3:5).

This second form of disintegration is more subtle and even more destructive. Those who take this route maintain what appears to be a vital, lively and growing spiritual pilgrimage. Like the church of Thyatira, they have "works . . . love and faith and service and patient endurance, and their latter works exceed the first" (Rev 2:19). But, like Thyatira, they seek to maintain an unholy mixture of faithful Christian discipleship and participation in the destructive brokenness of the world.[2] Their lives develop two radically different compartments. In one compartment is their spiritual pilgrimage, in the other their indulgent and disobedient participation in the brokenness of the world.

When we consider the consequences of one-sided spirituality, the need for holistic spirituality becomes all the more urgent.

Chapter 7
Holistic Spirituality

*O God of wholeness, when I consider the lack of balance and
wholeness in my life, the one-sided spiritualities with which I
attempt to appease you, to appear good in the eyes of others, and to
please myself, I come face to face with my need for a holistic spiritual life. Help me, I pray, to hunger and thirst for the wholeness
you have for me in Christ. Help me to be willing to surrender to
you whatever stands in the way of such wholeness.*

I am an INTJ. That means if there is to be holistic spiritual formation in my life, I need dynamics in my spiritual activities that will
nurture the ESFP part of me. For me, these become spiritual disciplines, because they are not activities that I would eagerly or naturally fall into. For instance, when in a chapel service at the seminary someone says, "Let's get together in groups of three or four
and share with one another something of what is going on in our
spiritual journey and pray together," I want to crawl under the pew.
This simply grates against my preference pattern. I most like chapel
when there is a period of silence and I can enter into my own world
of meditation and stillness. When I go to the monastery for a week-

end, that is a mountaintop experience for me. But to come to worship and be forced to be an ESFP is very difficult.

Yet I know I need it. If I do not nurture my less preferred side, that will cause problems with my whole spiritual pilgrimage.

The Center for Applications of Psychological Type has produced two charts, developed by Earle Page, that can help us see our need for a holistic spiritual journey.[1] The first is titled "Finding Your Spiritual Path."

It is of great value to reflect upon each segment of this chart, and I urge you to do so. See how well it fits your own preference patterns, but be alert to the note at the top of the chart: "These words are meant to suggest, not to define or to limit understanding." Given the wonderful diversity of our creation gifts, as we noted earlier, the correlation of these terms and phrases with any given individual will vary. Persons with a strong preference will probably find these indicators fairly accurate. Those with more nearly equal preferences between the pairs may find that the indicators do not fit them as well.

As you read down the column for each preference, you can see how that preference consistently shapes many areas of one's spiritual path. As we consider holistic spirituality, however, I would call your attention to the lines titled "Primary Arena" and "Natural Spiritual Path."

The primary arena of individuals' natural spiritual path depends upon their preference pattern. For extraverts, of course, it's the world and others. Their focus of attention is outward, and so their natural spiritual path is activity. These are people who by their works will manifest their faith. For introverts, the primary arena is ideas and self. Their center tends to be within, and their natural spiritual path is, consequently, reflective. For sensing persons the primary arena of the spiritual path is the body, because they rely on their senses for the primary data that they work with to relate to the world around them. Intuitive persons rely on the intuition

Table 1. Finding Your Spiritual Path

Note: These words are meant to suggest, not to define or to limit understanding.

Preferred Attitude, Function, or Lifestyle	Extraversion E	Introversion I	Sensing S	Intuition N	Thinking T	Feeling F	Judgment J	Perception P
Primary Arena	World/Other	Ideas/Self	Body	Spirit	Mind	Heart	Will	Awareness
Preference for	Action	Reflection	Sensory reality Details Status quo	Possibilities Patterns Change	Objective values	Subjective values	Initiative	Response
Significant Aspects of Reality	Exterior	Interior	Immediacy Concreteness	Anticipation Vision	Theory Principles	Feeling Memory Ideal	Product Categorical	Process Conditional
Windows Through Which God's Revelation Is Received	People Events Scripture Natural world	Individual experience Inspiration Inner world	Society Institutions "The Seen"	Insight Imagination "The Unseen"	Reason Speculation	Relationships Emotions	Order "Ought"	Serendipity "is"
Significant Aspects of God	Immanence Creator Imago Dei	Transcendence Identity of God and inner self	Incarnation	Mystery Holy Spirit	The Absolute Principle First Cause	Relational Familial (e.g. Father)	Judge Ruler	Redeemer Healer
Approach to Bible, Religious Experience	Social	Solitary	Practical Literal	Symbolic Metaphorical	Analytical Abstract	Personal Immediate	Systematic	Of-the-moment
Avoids (Hell)	Exclusion Loneliness	Intrusions Confusion	Ambiguity	Restriction Repetition	Inconsistency Ignorance	Conflict Estrangement	Helplessness Disorder	Regimentation Deadlines
Seeks (Heaven)	Participation Reunion	Incorporation Fulfillment	Physical harmony Faithfulness Obedience	Aesthetic harmony Mystical union	Conceptual harmony Enlightenment Justice, Truth	Personal harmony Communion Appreciation	Closure Productivity Work ethic	Openness Receptivity Play ethic
Prayer	Corporate	Private	Sensuous (eyes, ears, nose, hands, mouth)	Intuitive	Cognitive	Affective	Planned	Unplanned
Natural Spiritual Path	Action	Reflection	Service	Awareness	Knowledge	Devotion	Discipline	Spontaneity
Needed for Wholeness	Reflection	Action or Participation	Awareness or Understanding	Service or Embodiment	Devotion	Knowledge	Spontaneity	Discipline

Copyright 1982 Center for Applications of Psychological Type emerging from within their own spirits as their primary source of data, and thus awareness is their natural spiritual path. In a thinking person, of course, the primary arena is the mind, with knowledge as the natural spiritual path; in a feeling person the heart is the primary arena of the spiritual life, with devotion as the natural spiritual path. For persons whose preferred pattern is judgment, the exercise of the will is the primary arena of a natural spiritual path that manifests itself in a disciplined spirituality. For the person whose preference is perception, the primary arena is awareness, an openness and responsiveness to the ebb and flow of life around them, and this results in spontaneity as their natural spiritual path.

It is interesting to observe how these preferences manifest themselves in the body of Christ. You can almost always distinguish those who prefer judgment and those who prefer perception in a congregation. If the worship service is normally scheduled to close at noon, at about five minutes to twelve, the Js start looking at their watches. In cold weather, they will put their coats up over their shoulders and pull on their gloves. They are ready to go; they expect closure at twelve o'clock. The Ps, however, especially if the service is going well and the Lord has especially anointed the worship that Sunday, couldn't care less if the folks from all the other churches get to the restaurant before them. If the service went on to twelve-fifteen or twelve-thirty it wouldn't make much difference to them. The Js want closure, order, regularity, system. The Ps go with the flow; they move spontaneously with what is.

Those who prefer intuition, especially if they also have a preference for introversion, will be deeply enriched by periods of silence in worship, times for them to become reflective and enter into a deeper awareness of God's presence and the movements of the Spirit. For those who prefer extraversion and sensing, however, such spaces are uncomfortable voids that they will attempt to fill with some type of activity. Extravert-sensing people are enriched by a lively mode of worship that provides a high level of interaction with others and sensory input and output.

You can undoubtedly expand these illustrations by study of the chart and from your own experiences in the body of Christ. All of this reveals how our preferred patterns of being and doing deeply shape our individual and corporate spirituality.

Now, notice the bottom of the chart. Below the "natural spiritual path" we find what is needed for wholeness. The natural spiritual path for an extravert is action; for an introvert, it is reflection. But what does the extravert need for wholeness? Reflection! What does the introvert need for wholeness? Action or participation!

The pattern of reversal continues across the board: for the sensing preference the natural spiritual path is service; for the intuitive preference it is awareness. Each needs the opposite for wholeness; the same goes for thinking-feeling and judgment-perception.

Here is the crucial point: in order for our spiritual pilgrimage to be a balanced growth toward wholeness in the image of Christ for others, we need to have dynamics of spiritual life that will nurture both sides of our preference pattern.

In both our individual and corporate spirituality there need to be activities and disciplines that provide such balanced and holistic growth. Paul's word to the Corinthians becomes a reminder to us of our need for one another in our pilgrimage toward wholeness in Christ for others. The different members of the body bring to each other the strengths of their preference patterns as gifts of God's grace to those of different patterns. The ESFP is God's gift to the INTJ, and the INTJ is God's gift to the ESFP. They may be very uncomfortable gifts to each other, but the spiritual dynamics of the strength of each nurtures the weakness of the other.

A Balancing Act

The second chart (table 2) illustrates the need for balanced spirituality.

Note at the top and bottom lines the replication of the "natural

Table 2. Following Your Spiritual Path

Note: Our aim is a balanced, centered spirituality. These words are meant to facilitate understanding, not to stifle individuality.

Spiritual Path	Action E	Reflection I	Service S	Awareness N	Knowledge T	Devotion F	Discipline J	Spontaneity P
Some Positive Expressions	Assertiveness Building community	Independence Deepening community	Love Pleasure	Ecstasy Anticipation	Equanimity Objectivity	Compassion Rapport, Trust	Discrimination Competence	Acceptance Serenity
Some Negative Expressions	Anger Attack	Fear Withdrawal	Attachment	Elation Depression	Apathy Criticalness	Sentimentality Overprotectiveness	Inappropriate control Judging others	Failure to take responsibility
Underdevelopment May Lead to	Isolation Lack of circumspection	Emptiness Dependence	Abstraction Overlooking	Flatness	Confusion	Coldness Distrust	Loss of purpose Indecision	Premature closure Baseless conclusions
Overdevelopment May Lead to	Impatience Shallowness	Withholding Idiosyncrasy Inappropriate intensity	Idolatry Frivolity Inappropriate conformity	Illusion Impracticality Stubbornness Fickleness	Reductionism Cynicism Dogmatism Rumination	Credulity Personalizing Blaming	Rigidity Perfectionism	Passivity Impulsiveness Procrastination
Special Temptations and Vulnerabilities	Distraction Suggestibility	Inaction Inclusion by others	Superstition Suspicion Fear of change	Primitive sensuality Psychogenic illness	Emotional explosion, exploitation, indulgence Contaminated thinking	Idealizing authority Pseudo-objectivity Hurt feelings	Self-righteousness Scrupulosity	Rebelliousness Carelessness
Needed for Wholeness	Reflection	Action or Participation	Awareness	Service or Embodiment	Devotion	Knowledge	Spontaneity	Discipline

Copyright 1982 Center for Applications of Psychological Type spiritual path" and the transposition of what each preference needs for wholeness. Also note the "positive expressions" of the natural spiritual path for each preference. Again, remember that the terms and phrases are general representatives, not rigid guidelines.

The next four categories are most significant in helping us to see the dangers of one-sided spirituality and the urgent need for a balanced, holistic spiritual pilgrimage. Look at some of the negative expressions in following the spiritual path of your preferences. Some of the negative expressions for extraverts are anger and attack. Extraverts have their primary focus in the world, and when the world irritates them they will tend to respond in anger, attacking the cause of their difficulty. Introverts, however, whose primary focus is within, will tend to respond with fear and withdrawal, distancing themselves from the cause of their discomfort. For persons whose preference is judgment, a negative expression is inappropriate control or judging of others. This emerges from their desire to maintain control, to have closure, especially closure according to their own perspectives and purposes. By contrast, for persons whose preference is perception, a negative expression is failure to take responsibility. They can go with the flow to such an extent that they never take control. Study for yourself the S-N and T-F negative expressions, remembering that sensing persons prefer to rely on their physical senses for information and intuitives trust the inner movements of the spirit, while the thinking person processes life with the head and the feeling person with the heart.

The sections on underdevelopment, overdevelopment and special temptations and vulnerabilities are vitally important for our understanding of what may be some of the "besetting sins" and habitual failures of our spiritual journey, as well as for the crucial need for a balanced and holistic spirituality. Take intuitive-type persons. As I mentioned in the previous chapter, one particular temptation of intuitive persons is primitive sensuality. Can you see the rationale for this? If intuitives do not seek spiritual nurture of the sensing side of their nature, the sensing side will be deprived, starved, and it will cry out for nurture in unhealthy ways. The result may be primitive sensuality, the kinds of sexual exploits into which some leading Christian figures have fallen recently, or perhaps a more private obsession with sexual fantasies, pornography or masturbation. (Could it be that *extravert* intuitives will tend to express primitive sensuality with others, heightening the possibility of disclosure, while *introvert* intuitives will tend to express primitive sensuality privately and alone?) Another result may be psychogenic illness, actual physical symptoms of illness caused by psychological mechanisms, because they have not been nurturing the sensing side of their being.

Overdevelopment of the intuitive preference may lead to illusion, impracticality, stubbornness and fickleness: illusion if corrective data from the senses is ignored; impracticality if the intuition, without corrective input from the senses, becomes the basis for action; stubbornness if the impractical behavior is maintained in the face of corrective resistance from the world; fickleness if the person waffles between following intuition without correction and occasionally allowing the sensing side to have a corrective role.

With underdevelopment it is necessary, in each pair of preferences, to look at the opposite preference. Intuitive persons will tend to underdevelop their sensing side. This will result in abstraction, a view of the world that tends to overlook contrary data from the senses. Add each of the other preferences to this review of the intuitive, and you can appreciate the crucial need for wholeness in our spiritual life, to pursue spiritual dynamics that will feed the opposite side of our preference pattern. This is not to say that "unspiritual" behaviors and sinful attitudes and actions are simply a case of psychological imbalance that can be cured by nurturing the alternate side of the pair. Ultimately the issue is one of control. Who rules our heart with its desires and purposes—God or us?

The Need for Reflection

You may want to do some reflection on the nature of your spiritual life, what the patterns of your spirituality are, and to ask yourself the question "How do my patterns of individual and corporate spirituality nurture my shadow side?" We will focus on some of the specific disciplines of holistic spirituality in the next section, but each of us and each of our communities of faith need to intentionally offer to God spiritual disciplines and practices through which God can nurture us holistically toward wholeness in Christ for others.[2]

For instance, those involved in developing the worship patterns in a local congregation have an important responsibility. If the leader or leaders of the community of faith structure spiritual activities and worship in line with their preference patterns, any persons in the community who represent the alternate side of that pattern will have a sense of being spiritually marginalized and deprived. We tend to develop worship patterns that suit our own preferences. If the church stays with the same pattern of worship for ten or fifteen years, the result may be a congregation of people whose preference patterns are essentially the same. We should ensure that our corporate spirituality nurtures persons holistically. The same holds true for small groups, which often stagnate in a pattern of spirituality that is comfortable for the members but restrictive to potential new members whose presence might be a much-needed gift of God's grace to the group.

In our corporate spirituality, there should be elements of interaction with others balanced with space for individual reflection; worshiping God with our bodies and senses balanced with opportunities to listen and respond to the whispers of the Spirit; loving God with our minds by careful thinking upon the issues of our discipleship as the body of Christ in the world and loving God with our hearts through affective responses to God and others; an orderly and disciplined liturgy balanced by openness to the movement of God's Spirit.

The goal of a holistic spiritual pilgrimage is related to all we have been saying about the creation gifts of our psychological makeup. Our spiritual formation always takes place within our given psychological state and personality preference pattern. These dynamics are always modulating. Our preference patterns don't change all that much; by the time we reach adulthood, our preference patterns are fairly well established. But our psychological state is always in modulation. The process of being conformed to the image of Christ for others is always uniquely related at any given moment to where we are in these two continuities: our personality preference pattern and our psychological state. We need to be sensitive to this. If we are not, our spirituality will tend to be very superficial most of our lives.

In fact, this is what has happened to spirituality in many parts of the Christian church. Our spirituality is very weakly tied to the realities of our daily existence. We tend to become dualistic—spiritual life on one side and the rest of life on the other. I believe this is because we have not realized how deeply our spiritual life and growth into wholeness—genuine spirituality—is interwoven with the dynamics of our being and doing. This makes holistic spirituality a much more complex thing than perhaps we want to deal with. It is so much easier to seek the right trick, the right method, the right technique, to give us the level of spirituality we desire at a minimum of cost and with a minimal disruption to the normal flow of life.

I hope the overview given in this chapter has enabled you to understand something of the nature of your own spiritual journey, perhaps to realize the cause of some of the problems you have been having, and to be alert to the need for balance in your spiritual pilgrimage.

We have now considered the vehicle in which we make our spiritual journey toward wholeness in the image of Christ for the sake of others. It is time to consider the journey itself.

Part III
The Journey:
Spiritual Disciplines

T
he Christian's journey toward wholeness in the image of
Christ for the sake of others progresses by means of spiritual
disciplines. Just as a journey from one place to another requires varied sets of disciplines for successful completion (walking,
driving, flying, navigation skills and the like), so the Christian journey has its own sets of disciplines which enable the pilgrim to progress through the stages of the spiritual path toward wholeness in
Christ. In this section four aspects of the spiritual pilgrimage will
be developed.

In the first chapter of the section (chapter eight), we will examine
the stages of the classical Christian journey. These stages are
generally called awakening, purgation, illumination and union.
These are the stages that move us from our separation and alien-
ation from God, our unlikeness to the image of Christ, to transforming relationship with God and wholeness in Christ.

Awakening occurs whenever we encounter and respond to God at
some point of our unlikeness to Christ. *Purgation* is the process that
deals with our areas of unlikeness to Christ. *Illumination* is the emer-
gence of a new being that begins to manifest something of the
image of Christ in the world. *Union* is the experience of wholeness
in union with God.

In the second chapter of this section (chapter nine), the classical disciplines of the Christian journey will be probed: prayer, spiritual reading, liturgy. The classical disciplines, in one sense, form the "roadbed" on which we move through the stages of the journey. Or, to use another image, they are the guardrails that keep the vehicle of our being on the road that leads us through the stages of the pilgrimage toward wholeness in the image of Christ. These classical disciplines will also be seen as the larger matrix within which other very specific and personal disciplines are to be offered to God as an exercise of faith and a means of grace. They can be viewed as the scaffolding within which the reconstruction of our life toward wholeness takes place.

The classical disciplines of the spiritual pilgrimage are the practices that the church has come to realize are essential for deepening one's relationship with God, enriching one's life with others and nurturing one toward wholeness in Christ. While the classical disciplines, such as prayer, Bible reading, worship, study, fasting, retreat and daily office, have both personal and corporate dimensions, the personal disciplines are acts of loving obedience by which we offer our brokenness and bondage to God for healing and liberation. Such disciplines are uniquely shaped to the form of our personal unlikeness to Christ; an example of a personal discipline would be the commitment to abstain from indulging in something that had been destroying us.

Without the classical disciplines, personal disciplines can quickly become privatized and even pathological—privatized in the sense of keeping our relationship with God firmly under our control and permitting us to adjust the call to discipleship to fit our agenda, our likes and dislikes, our wants and wishes; pathological in the sense of a spirituality that binds us to inadequate or destructive responses to life. Without personal disciplines, on the other hand, the classical disciplines can quickly become a debilitating façade that covers one's deep needs for transformation.

The third chapter in this section (chapter ten) will describe and illustrate the character of personal spiritual disciplines. I put special emphasis, however, on the corporate dimension of personal disciplines. There is no way that an individual can be conformed to the image of Christ for others without the nurture of the body of Christ; and there is no way that the community of faith can be the body of Christ if it does not nurture the individual members toward wholeness in Christ.

The final chapter (eleven) will examine the classical personal disciplines of silence, solitude and prayer. The profound dimensions of these practices as the essence of our personal spiritual disciplines will be examined, and they will be seen as the means by which we journey from awakening through purgation to illumination and union.

Chapter 8
The Classical
Christian Pilgrimage

*O God, I feel like Abraham must have felt when he started his
journey of obedience to you, not knowing where he was going. I am
uncomfortable not having control of my itinerary, not being able to
choose the route. While my present state of brokenness and
incompleteness is not always pleasant or comfortable, at least I am
accustomed to it and know my way around in it. Help me to let
you lead me out into the unknown; overcome my fear with your
love, my hesitancy with your hope for my wholeness.*

———————

The classical pilgrimage toward wholeness in Christ has been
characterized by four stages. These can be thought of either as the
overall path of Christian spirituality through life or as the path
toward wholeness in any given area of our lives. That is, all four
of these stages can take place incrementally within our spiritual
pilgrimage and, at the same time, shape the whole pilgrimage itself.
For instance, the movement from awakening through purgation
and illumination to union describes the general path of the lifelong
pilgrimage that begins when we awaken to God's call to wholeness
and "ends" in an eternal life in relationship with God. The move-

ment can also describe the more particular path we experience in a given area of our unlikeness to Christ: God calls us out of that unlikeness (awakening) and moves us to an increasing relinquishment of that unlikeness (purgation); this leads to a new structure of being and doing (illumination) and eventually culminates in Christlikeness of spirit and behavior at that particular point of our life (union).

This means that we can be at different stages in various areas. In one area we may be well along the path to wholeness, while in another area God is just beginning to awaken us to another part of our life that needs transformation. Since God always leaves us free to reject transformation, it is also possible for us to regress in this process, or, in old-fashioned terms, to backslide. Thus our Christian pilgrimage is a complex, multifaceted, multilevel ebb and flow of relationship with God.

It might be helpful to chart the classical Christian pilgrimage and its components before we begin to examine it more closely. Consider table 3 on the following page.

Awakening

The first stage is *awakening*. Holistic spiritual awakening is a two-sided experience. It is an encounter with the living God; it is also an encounter with our true self. It is coming to see something of ourselves as we are and coming to see something of God as God is.

This experience can be gradual or radical. It can take place through everyday events or in an extraordinary experience. It can be one focal experience or a whole sequence that finally falls together for us. On some occasions, moments of awakening begin with an experience of who God is, such as Isaiah's—"I saw the Lord sitting upon a throne, high and lifted up" (Is 6:1). Then, in the light of that experience, we awake to who we are—"Woe is me! . . . I am a man of unclean lips" (Is 6:5). On other occasions, like Jacob, we

Table 3. The Classical Christian Pilgrimage

The Stages	Their Aspects
Awakening	Encounter with God Encounter with self Comfort Threat
Purgation	Renunciation of blatant sins Renunciation of willful disobedience Unconscious sins and omissions Deep-seated structures of being and behavior Coming to trust
Illumination	Total consecration to God in love God experienced within Integration of being Unceasing prayer Increasing social concern
Union	Abandonment to Grace Prayer of quietness Dark night of the senses Full union/ecstatic union Dark night of the spirit

may be very much aware of who we are as we seek to escape from the mess we have made of our life (Gen 27:41-44). Then we encounter God in the midst of our turmoil—"Surely the LORD is in this place, and I did not know it" (Gen 28:16). Awakening can come in a variety of ways.

Two basic emotions go with awakening: it is both a *comfort* and a *threat.* It is comfort because there is a sense of awakening to deeper realities of who we are and who God is. But at the same time there is threat: in that awakening, we recognize that we are not what we ought to be and that God is something far more than we thought. And so there is an ambivalence in genuine awakening. Something in us hungers for this, yet something in us also resists.

Genuine awakening is the awareness of a door being opened to a whole new dynamic of being. We realize we have come to a threshold of some sort, and there is need of a response. Our response may be immediate, or it may come after much wrestling and recurrence. Some people are aroused into the early stages of wakefulness and then quickly subside into sleep. They don't like what is out there. It is not time to get up yet. They will be roused up again and lie back down again, and that pattern can continue until finally they come to the point of awakening: they step across the threshold of the open door into a new relationship with God.

Awakening is seen in the classical Christian tradition as the beginning of the process: the first step of our journey, our pilgrimage, toward wholeness.

Purgation

The next stage is *purgation:* the process of bringing our behavior, our attitudes, our desires into increasing harmony with our growing perception of what the Christlike life is all about. Here is where the classical spiritual disciplines and the personal spiritual disciplines we will consider in the next chapters come primarily into play, although the disciplines also engender constant awakenings, deepen the stage of illumination and shape the experience of union with God. Purgation is the process of becoming integrated into the new order of being in Christ.

Purgation has its own stages. First of all, there is a renunciation of all blatant inconsistencies with wholeness in Christ—what the fathers and mothers of the Christian spiritual tradition call "gross sins." We begin to bring our life under the values of God's kingdom, abandoning behaviors that are contrary to God's will as revealed in

Christ and Scripture—for example, Paul's list in Galatians: "fornication, impurity, licentiousness, idolatry, sorcery, enmity, strife, jealousy, anger, selfishness, dissension, party spirit, envy, drunkenness, carousing" (Gal 5:19-21). This stage of purgation deals with aspects of our old life that are clearly and unmistakably inconsistent with God's will for our wholeness. Often we are aware of these aspects of our life even before awakening comes to call us to purgation. Many of these behaviors are even suspect in the eyes of the world.

Then purgation moves to other deliberate sins of our life—what Wesley called "willful transgressions of the known will of God." In this stage, purgation leads us to deal with behaviors that may be "normal" and "acceptable" in our culture but which the Scripture and the Spirit of God tell us are not part of God's will for our wholeness. For instance, Scripture's norms for sexual behavior are much more stringent than those of our culture.

Some of the behaviors dealt with at this stage, however, may not be inherently bad. They may even be biblically acceptable, but not for my own pilgrimage. Paul recognizes this reality in the issue of eating meat. One person's faith allows him to eat everything, but another person eats only vegetables (Rom 14:2). Paul says, "The one who eats everything must not look down on the one who does not, and the one who does not eat everything must not condemn the one who does" (Rom 14:3). Yet Paul tells the Corinthians, "If what I eat causes my brother or sister to fall into sin, I will never eat meat again, so that I will not cause them to fall" (1 Cor 8:13).

While the issue of eating meat may be irrelevant for our day, the principle is clear: there is the possibility that a behavior that is destructive of one person's spiritual growth may be acceptable for another. But we must never let our behavior become a hindrance to the pilgrimage of our sisters or brothers in Christ. It is in such areas that we are tempted to rationalize our behavior and provide ourselves with good excuses for doing evil or avoiding good, especially in a culture of moral relativism.

Next, purgation probes the unconscious sins and omissions of our life. This seems to be what Paul describes when, as one who "delights in the law of God in his inmost being" (Rom 7:22), he says, "I don't do the good I want, but the evil I don't want is what I do" (Rom 7:19). Here is where we begin to let the Spirit of God reveal to us aspects of our inner being that have been invisible to our view but that now we begin to see as hindrances to our growth toward wholeness in the image of Christ. God is very gracious in revealing these things to us, not all at once, but only as we are able to deal with them. Fénelon, the seventeenth-century spiritual master, put it well:

A traveller who is marching across a vast plain sees nothing ahead of him but a slight rise which ends the distant horizon. When he tops this rise, he finds a new stretch of country as vast as the first. Thus, in the way of self-renunciation, we think we see everything at once. We think that we are holding nothing back, and that we are not clinging to ourselves or to anything else. We should rather die than hesitate to make a complete sacrifice. But, in the daily round, God constantly shows us new countries. We find in our hearts a thousand things which we would have sworn were not there. God only shows them to us as he makes them appear. It is like an abscess which bursts. The moment when it bursts is the only one which horrifies us. Before that we were carrying it without feeling it, and we did not think we had it. However, we did have it, and it only broke because we had it. When it was hidden, we thought that we were healthy and quite as we should be. When it breaks we smell the stench of the pus. The breaking is healthy, although it is painful and disgusting. Each of us carries in the depth of his heart a mass of filth, which would make us die of shame if God should show us all its poison and horror. Self-love would be in an unbearable suffering. I am not speaking now of those whose hearts are gangrenous with enormous vices. I am speaking of the souls which seem honest and pure. We should see a foolish vanity which does not dare to come out in the open, and which stays in shame in the deepest folds of the heart. We should see self-complacencies, heights of pride, subtle selfishness, and a thousand windings within, which are as real as they are inexplicable. We only see them as God begins to make them emerge.[1]

At this stage God begins the process of disclosing to us those deep festering sores of our being in order that we may offer them up to God through the disciplines into which we have been led for their healing.

Finally, purgation deals with the deep-seated attitudes and inner orientations of our being out of which our behavior patterns flow. Here purgation deals essentially with our "trust structures," especially those deep inner postures of our being that do not rely on God but on self for our well-being. Catholic theologian and psychologist Benedict Groeschel characterizes this dimension of purgation as coming to mature faith and entering into the relationship of radical trust in God.[2] He describes mature faith as a decline of anxiety and an increase of peace. It is most interesting that Paul brings these two elements together in Philippians 4:6-7: "Have no anxiety about anything. . . . And the peace of God, which passes all understanding, will keep your hearts and minds in Christ Jesus."

This passage begins with Paul's exhortation to "rejoice always" (4:4).[3] Paul's global terms are always disconcerting. "Rejoice *always*"? "Have no anxiety about *anything*"? Isn't that carrying hyperbole a little far? Why not simply exhort us to "rejoice" and "be not anxious" and leave it at that? Then we could use our own discriminating judgment as to which situations called for rejoicing and which called for anxiety. To be so dogmatically inclusive is simply unrealistic in the kind of world we live in.

If we reflect further on Paul's exhortation to the Philippians, however, we find Paul saying, "I have learned in whatever state I am to be content. I know how to be abased, and I know how to abound; in any and all circumstances I have learned the secret of facing plenty and hunger, abundance and want" (Phil 4:11-12). This can be dismissed as pious theologizing until we realize that this is written by a person sitting in a Roman dungeon, not sure whether he will emerge alive (Phil 1:12-13). It would appear that Paul is not expounding theory but exhibiting a truth he has learned through years of faithful discipleship. Paul provides here not the argument for trust but the anatomy of trust.

The Futility of Anxious Care
If Paul characterizes trust by the victorious exhilaration of rejoicing, its opposite is a fretful and debilitating concern for one's own welfare—anxiety. "Rejoice . . . always" is paralleled by "In nothing be anxious." The two expressions are synonymous. Biblically, anxiety and care are symptoms of a failure of trust (see Mt 6:25-34).

Care arises when we are driven by the need to order and control our own lives. In a world where such order and control are partial at best, anxious care can become a consuming passion that misshapes all relationships, all events and all activities of one's life. When this happens, anxiety-driven persons tend to become manipulative and dehumanizing in their relationships with others. Others must conform to their pathological attempts to order the world and maintain control of their lives. Anxiety-driven persons are also compelled to impose their own order upon the events of their lives. Layer upon layer of defenses and securities are constructed to keep the unpredictable and unexpected from intruding into their carefully ordered world.

Such persons cannot be the persons God intends them to be. They are imprisoned by the need to maintain control of their existence. Such persons cannot be God's persons for others. They are captive to the need to protect themselves against others and manipulate others for their own purposes. Such persons cannot be agents of God's grace to a broken and hurting world. They are in bondage to the need to impose their order upon the world.

The most tragic aspect of this carefully crafted matrix of relationships and activities is that it also insulates one from God. In fact, in such lives God most often becomes one more element in the attempt to coerce the world to conform to protective patterns. God becomes not only the defender of the status quo but also, and usually, its reputed author. Anyone or anything that threatens the fragile order and control of life is obviously an enemy of God.

Such lives, closed within the fragile shell of their own limited order and control, are plagued with stress, anxiety, fear, doubt, despair, depression and a legion of other destructive and debilitating demons. Tense and troubled, such persons expend prodigious amounts of energy to maintain and defend their tenuous control of their lives—energies that could have graced healing and wholeness to a broken and hurting world.

A Radical Alternative

Paul bears witness to a radical alternative to such an anxious, tense, stress-filled and destructive existence. This alternative, however, does not shield us from the uncertainties of life. It does not protect us from life's damaging blows and disruptive events. It does not exempt us, in Paul's words, from being held in disrepute, from being hungry and thirsty, ill-clad, buffeted and homeless, from being persecuted and slandered, from being treated as the dust and dirt of the world (1 Cor 4:10-13). But it does empower us to learn, in Paul's words, to be content in any situation, knowing how to face plenty and hunger, abundance and want.

The general shape of Paul's anatomy of trust is found in the exhortation "Rejoice in the Lord." But this expression is capable of being badly misconstrued. It can be viewed as an escapist mode by which the person who is troubled and distressed by life's adversities escapes into a protective cocoon and retreats from all responsibility and involvement in troubling, distressing circumstances. It can be viewed in a manipulative mode by which the individual uses the "magical" method of rejoicing to get God to resolve all the disturbing conditions. It can be viewed in a repressive mode by which overstressed persons hide their turmoil and frustration behind a façade of "rejoicing."

Paul is calling us to something radically different from such inadequate responses to events that threaten our tenuous control of life. What Paul means by "Rejoice in the Lord" is seen in the injunction "Let all persons know your forbearance" (Phil 4:5). The Greek term translated "forbearance" conveys the idea of living according to an established structure of reality in the face of alternatives, especially threatening ones.[4] Paul is indicating that Christ's disciples live their lives within a particular order of being—one whose structures of character and dynamics of being transcend destructive events. This is not an escapist transcendence. It is the transcendence of a deeper order that embraces our tenuous and fragile world order and incorporates its disruption, even its destruction, into an eternal wholeness. It is the deeper order revealed in the incarnation, an order that accepts crucifixion and transforms its death into eternal life.

Paul indicates the nature of that established structure of reality by which we are to live in the midst of life's adversities when he writes, "The Lord is at hand" (Phil 4:5 RSV). Paul is not calling on Christians simply to hold on because the end of the world is at hand. He is indicating that Christ is the matrix of Christian existence in the world. This is what Paul affirms in such statements as "It is no longer I who live, but Christ who lives in me" (Gal 2:20 RSV) and "For me to live is Christ" (Phil 1:21 RSV). Paul conveys the same reality when he exhorts believers to "put on the Lord Jesus Christ" (Rom 13:14 RSV), the "new nature" (Eph 4:24 RSV), and indicates that all of us who were baptized into Christ have "put on Christ" (Gal 3:27 RSV).

This is the basis of the Christian's "forbearance" in the presence of situations that threaten our control of our lives and disrupt our ordered existence. The Christian's identity and value do not reside in the fragile order and tenuous control that she or he imposes upon life. Identity and value are found in a vital and living relationship with Christ as Lord. This relationship liberates Christians from dependence upon their little systems of order and fragile structures of control. Not that believers live without order or control, but they are liberated from dependency on those systems and structures for their sense of self.

Such a life of rejoicing in the Lord and "letting all know our forbearance" does not mean that Christians do not experience loss, pain and grief at the disruption or destruction of their order and control. They may feel such loss even more deeply, because each loss recalls them to the deeper loss of themselves for Christ's sake that is the recurrent theme and action of genuine discipleship. We do attach ourselves to our little systems of control, we do cling to our precious ordering of life. But the breaking of these attachments recalls us to our true attachment to Christ.

I will never forget an experience I had with a person who had learned Paul's lessons to rejoice always and to be anxious in nothing. Her pastor asked me to visit her for him, since she was to have surgery the next morning and he couldn't get over to the hospital due to a meeting. She was a wife and the mother of two children, in her early thirties, suffering from virulent diabetes that had already taken one leg and her eyesight. She was now facing the loss of her other leg. As I entered the hospital, I wondered to myself, *How in the world can I minister to someone who is suffering as she is?*

When I entered her room, she asked me if I would stand between her and the window so she could see my silhouette against the sunlight. She could still distinguish light from darkness. As I began to talk with her, I discovered a person whose deep inner peace gave a radiance to her whole being. There was no bitterness, no anger, no recrimination, no lashing out at God or others for her condition. She had learned truly to rest the entire weight of her being in God, to be anxious in nothing and to rejoice in everything. Instead of my ministering to her, she ministered to me, and I left that room knowing I had been in the presence of one of God's great ones.

Having set forth the general form of the anatomy of trust, Paul portrays the members of that anatomy—prayer, supplication, thanksgiving, petition (Phil 4:6). By these activities Paul brings our focus to the practices of rejoicing and forbearance.

The Human Action
At first glance, Paul seems to give us a list of synonyms. Are *prayer, supplication* and *petition* not all variant terms for the same basic action? Not quite. *Prayer (proseuche)* seems to be Paul's term for the deep inner posture of one's being toward God in open receptivity and pliable responsiveness. It is the term he uses when he exhorts us to "pray constantly" (1 Thess 5:17 RSV), to "continue steadfastly in prayer" (Col 4:2 RSV), to "be constant in prayer" (Rom 12:12 RSV). Praying without ceasing obviously presumes an inner posture of being for its fulfillment, a posture that undergirds all the activities and relationships of life. With this term Paul seems to call us not to isolated actions but to a habitual orientation of our being toward God at the deepest levels. This is an inner discipline of life which, in every circumstance, leads the heart to "swing like the needle, to the polestar of the soul."[5]

Supplication reminds us of the nature of a suppliant—one who recognizes his or her condition of inadequacy and impotence, an utter inability to provide what is needed. With this, the suppliant also acknowledges the adequacy, power and ability of the one whose aid is sought. Paul seems to call us, in the midst of life's disruptions of our order and control, to a consistent acknowledgment of the insufficiency of our resources and the inadequacy of our ability to maintain order and control in the face of the world's wildness. He calls us to be continually turned to God as the source of our sufficiency in every circumstance. Prayer and supplication, then, are not reactions to circumstances; they are the habits of the heart by which we meet the troublesome events of life.

Having established the posture of the disciple's heart toward God in the midst of life's disruptions, Paul speaks of our *petitions*. These requests, however, are now set within a different frame of reference. If we have not first entered into the posture of prayer and supplication, our requests tend to be very narrowly focused upon our own agenda and have their center in our self-referenced matrix of life. The posture of prayer and supplication, however, places us and our situations into the deeper matrix of God's presence and purpose. While still shaped by our perception of the situation, our requests begin to become the bridge between our own desires and the purposes of God. When this happens, our requests become the practice of forbearance. We begin to place the situations of our lives into the deeper matrix of God's presence and purpose and find that we can release our tenuous control and fragile ordering of life to God.

Paul describes the inner current of forbearance when he indicates that our requests are to be made with thanksgiving. This is not a magical formula that guarantees God's hearing and response. It is not a way of manipulating God to solve the problem in our way. Thanksgiving is the deep inner posture of joyful release of our life and being to God in absolute trust, without demands, without conditions, without reservations. If Paul's call to forbearance is actualized by our requests in a posture of prayer and supplication, thanksgiving fulfills his call to rejoice in the Lord. Thus Paul's anatomy of trust comes full circle.

The Divine Response

But Paul is not finished. He has described only the human side of the anatomy of trust. There is also God's side. When this mode of trust characterizes our life with God in the world, then the peace of God that passes all understanding keeps our hearts and minds in Christ Jesus (Phil 4:7).

The first thing to note is that the peace of God is not a static concept; it is an active reality. God's peace, God's *shalom*, is a vital relationship with God in which we find the true fulfillment of our being, true identity and value. This relationship is a living and active reality that shapes and guides the life of the disciple who lives in the kind of trust Paul has described.

Perhaps an example can be drawn from musicianship. One violinist may be a master technician who plays a concerto with such flawless technical perfection that the audience is astounded at his dexterity. Another violinist, however, perhaps with less technical skill, allows the music to be played through her in a way that transports the audience to experience the music itself rather than simply appreciate a performance.

The trust to which Paul calls us is a giving of ourselves to God so that God can be "played" through our lives in whatever circumstances we encounter. When God is released in our lives in this way, our lives are held in the flow of God's presence and purpose.

This experience cannot be grasped by finite human understanding. If we could grasp it, we could also control it and order it according to our own desires for the threatening and disrupting circumstances of our lives. We would become the technicians performing the music. Instead, Paul tells us, trust is a release of both mind and heart to God. This trust is what the classical Christian tradition calls *detachment*. It is neither a passive resignation nor a fatalistic acquiescence to whatever comes. It is, rather, a consistent posture of actively turning our whole being to God so that God's presence, purpose and power can be released through our lives into all situations.

The Life of Trust

Such trust liberates us to be the persons God calls us to be in the world. Without such trust, our lives are imprisoned within the protective shells of our tenuous order and control. Such trust enables us to be God's persons for others. Without such trust, our lives are spent defending ourselves against the real or imagined threats of others, or manipulating others for our own purposes. Such trust empowers us to be agents of God's transforming grace in a hurting and broken world. Without such trust, we are unable to stand against the systemic evil of institutions and society.

Only in the context of an inner orientation of life that rests the whole weight of its being in God's presence and purpose can Paul's "always" statements make any sense. Only in such a context can we rejoice always and be anxious in nothing.

This yieldedness to God is the "trust" Groeschel describes as the deepest of the stages of purgation. It is trust that rests one's being totally and completely in God's love and care without demands, conditions or prior expectations. Even in the darkness of God's seeming absence, trust rests the weight of one's being absolutely in God. The psalmist captures this deep inner posture of trust in Psalm 131:

O Lord, my heart is not proud
    nor haughty my eyes.
I have not gone after things too great
    nor marvels beyond me.
Truly I have set my soul
    in silence and peace.
A weaned child on its mother's breast,
    even so is my soul.[6]

The first affirmation expresses the absence of self-concerned anxiety. Then, in the image of the weaned child at its mother's breast, the psalmist reveals the life of absolute trust in God. The *unweaned* child is at its mother's breast for its own needs, its own agenda—milk. The weaned child, however, has no such need or agenda. It is content to rest in the mother's arms and receive whatever attention she chooses to give.

The stage of purgation is characterized by the struggle of two selves: the self that is not yet all that it has been created to be in God's will for our wholeness, and the wholeness of self that God holds out before us. The old, anxious, egocentric self is called to increasing mortification in order that the new, peace-filled, God-centered self may come more and more into being.

Illumination

The third stage, *illumination*, is characterized by a radical shift of the deep dynamics of our being, a profound transformation of our relationship with God. Illumination is the experience of total consecration to God in love. Rather than my being in charge of my relationship with God, God is given absolute control of the relationship. This is what Wesley described as "Christian perfection."

The apostle John saw something of this reality of the Christian pilgrimage in his vision of the worship of the elders (Rev 4:10). The twenty-four elders, who represent the covenant community of God's people,[7] are seen bowing before God's throne, worshiping and casting their crowns before God. In the imagery of that day, bowing acknowledged the authority of the one before whom one bowed. The bowing of the elders represents awakening to God and acknowledgment of God as God. The worship of the elders can, in some sense, represent purgation, the process of allowing God to rule in one's life in areas where self has ruled before. In one sense, the most vital and genuine worship of God is bringing our lives into harmony with God's will. How often is our formal worship merely an attempt to appease God for lives that are lived essentially with no real reference to God's purposes? God speaks of such behavior through Isaiah:

When you come to appear before me,
   who requires of you
   this trampling of my courts?
Bring no more vain offerings;

incense is an abomination to me.
New moon and sabbath and the calling of assemblies—
I cannot endure iniquity and solemn assembly. (Is 1:12-13)

The casting of the crowns (an image of authority and control) represents illumination, the continual and consistent yielding the control of one's life totally and completely to God.

Illumination is characterized by a number of things. The basic shift in illumination is from seeing God as "out there" to an experience of God present deep within our being. This goes hand in hand with the deep level of absolute trust to which the purgative stage brings us. As long as God is perceived as "out there," separated from us, we understand ourselves as independent, autonomous beings. We labor under the anxiety that causes us to attempt to retain control of our relationship with God and to control our limited world. The peace that keeps our hearts and minds surpasses this type of self-understanding (Phil 4:7). Such peace is a deep integration of our being that comes from the release of ourselves to God, that illumines us to the presence of God within. The Trappist monk Thomas Merton puts it like this:

We awaken not only to a realization of the immensity and majesty of God "out there" as King and Ruler of the universe (which He is) but also a more intimate and more wonderful perception of Him as directly and personally present in our own being. Yet this is not a pantheistic merger or confusion of our being with His. On the contrary, there is a distinct conflict in the realization that though in some sense He is more truly ourselves then we are, yet we are not identical with Him, and though He loves us better than we can love ourselves we are opposed to Him, and in opposing Him we oppose our own deepest selves. If we are involved only in our surface existence, in externals, and in the trivial concerns of our ego, we are untrue to Him and to ourselves. To reach a true awareness of Him as well as ourselves, we have to renounce our selfish and limited self and enter into a whole new kind of existence, discovering an inner center of motivation and love which makes us see ourselves and everything else in an entirely new light.[8]

In this stage, prayer becomes the flow of our life as God is experienced in all things. I think what Paul speaks of as unceasing prayer is a life that is increasingly attuned to God in all things—not in a privatized withdrawal from the world, but in the midst of the hustle and bustle, busyness and pain, hurt and brokenness of our life and the world around us.

As God becomes a vital and living reality in our own being, God, paradoxically, also becomes more present in the world "out there," infusing all things, events, persons with the fullness of God's presence and purpose. There emerges a new connectedness between our relationship with God and our relationship with the world. The growing experience of inner, silent adoration of God at the heart of our being moves us to the offering of ourselves to God for others. It is at this point that what Groeschel calls "infused virtues"[9]—empowerment by God for holy living in the world—enable us to meet the world compassionately, creatively, transformingly, redemptively.

Such empowerment is what Paul describes as the fruits of the Spirit: love, joy, peace, patience, kindness, goodness, faithfulness, gentleness, self-control (Gal 5:22-23 RSV). These come not by our effort nor by attempts to inculcate them in our actions, but are gifts that emerge as we release control of our lives and come to entrust ourselves to God.

Illumination is also characterized by increasing social concern, not out of obligation but out of a deep sense of God's love poured into our hearts for others. Good works are a hallmark of the illuminative way, not as a responsibility or a duty but, again, as a response of love. What happens in illumination is a paradigm shift in our motivation. Rather than a self-referenced, self-concerned motivation for our relationship with God, our motivation becomes a heart burning with love for God, the opening of our very being to the One whom we love, and living our life in the world out of that love.

But the stage of illumination is not some idyllic life free from problems. Groeschel paints a potent image of this stage of the Christian pilgrimage: "The illuminative way is not a cloudless summer day. It is a spring morning after a bad storm. Even though everything is washed clean and the sky is filled with clouds and sunlight, there are many fallen trees and an occasional live wire blocking the road."[10] It is possible for us to succumb to pride and self-righteousness, to think of ourselves as set apart from others by a special call, to develop spiritual greed—desiring the riches of God for our own pleasure and enjoyment. The French writer Adolphe Tanquerey provides an uncomfortable list of signs of a bad spirit: "to practice showy virtues . . . contempt for little things and the desire to be sanctified in a grand manner . . . false humility . . . false meekness . . . to complain, to lose patience."[11]

Illumination is a life of deep sensitivity and responsiveness to the presence of God deep within our being and at the heart of the life of the world around us.

Union

The final stage of the Christian pilgrimage is called *union*. It is also known by such terms as *spiritual marriage, transforming union, ecstasy, the unitive way* and *contemplation*. It characterizes those experiences of complete oneness with God in which we find ourselves caught up in rapturous joy, adoration, praise and a deep peace that passes all understanding. This is a gift of God's grace—not the result of our efforts. As Groeschel says, "One accepts it, but in no way does one cause it."[12] Of course, without the deep inner desire to be abandoned to God, one will hardly ever come to such a depth of relationship with God, even though, as the traditional catechism tells us, this is the goal of our existence—to enjoy God forever.

But union is not an escapist kind of experience. It is the experi-

ence of being at last in the kind of relationship with God for which
we were created and for which our beings yearn. Merton puts it like
this:

It is the gift of God Who, in His mercy, completes the hidden and
mysterious work of creation in us by enlightening our minds and
hearts, by awakening in us the awareness that we are words
spoken in His One Word, and that Creating Spirit *(Creator Spiritus)*
dwells in us, and we in Him. That we are "in Christ" and that
Christ lives in us. That the natural life in us has been completed,
elevated, transformed and fulfilled in Christ by the Holy Spirit.
Contemplation is the awareness and realization, even in some
sense *experience*, of what each Christian obscurely believes: "It is
now no longer I that live but Christ lives in me."[13]

As long as we try to fill this yearning with things other than God
and activities other than God's purposes, we are unfulfilled and
incomplete.

As with some of the other stages of the Christian pilgrimage,
union has several components. Relying upon St. John of the Cross
and St. Teresa of Ávila, the two greatest writers on this stage,
Groeschel lists the components of union as prayer of quietness,
dark night of the senses, full union with God, ecstatic union, dark
night of the spirit and transforming union.[14]

The *prayer of quietness* is a posture of yieldedness to God's presence
and purpose, a purity of intention that brings, in Groeschel's words,
"great control and mastery over [our] behavior."[15] The holistic nature of this experience is beautifully captured by Groeschel, who
says, "Watching a person in the unitive way is like watching a great
musician playing an instrument on which he or she has complete
mastery and control."[16] We might add to this image the idea that
the person in such union not only lives with complete mastery over
the "instrument" of his or her life but also sounds forth in all beauty
and fullness the harmonies of God's purposes into the world.

In the *dark night of the senses* the last remaining dependencies upon intellectual and emotional feedback are painfully surrendered. We depend upon cognitive assent and affective assurances to substantiate the reality of our relationship with God. If we can't "know" or "feel" God, we customarily doubt our relationship with God. But such "knowing" and "feeling" restrict God to the narrow limits of our minds and senses and reduce our relationship with God to the maintenance of such feedback. The dark night of the senses begins to move us beyond such dependency to an unconditioned relationship with God. Groeschel notes that this is often a time of great suffering: "a mysterious collection of misfortunes overtakes people at this time."[17] The biblical model here is Job, who, deprived of all affective and cognitive assurances of God's love and care, comes to the deep experience of God that transcends such assurances. This is heavy stuff! But ultimately God must be in our life who God is, unrestricted by the narrow limits of our thought or feeling.

In *full union*, "between the movement of the human mind and will and the loving designs of God there is complete harmony . . . the absolute certitude of God's presence in the soul."[18] It is what Hildegard of Bingen pictured so beautifully as being a feather on the breath of God, or what St. Catherine of Genoa describes in this way: "God busies the soul with Himself, in no matter how slight a way, and the soul, wrapped up in God, cannot but be oblivious to all else."[19] As Groeschel notes, "persons at this level no longer experience the need for human reinforcement and approval, they are quiet and gentle and very unobtrusive."[20]

Such a pliability in God's hands is, in the mystical tradition of Christian spirituality, occasionally accompanied by the experience of ecstasy, or *ecstatic union*, best described as a period of total absorption[21] in God during which a person is unaware of her or his surroundings. Paul's description of being caught up to the third heaven, where he didn't know whether he was in the body or out of the body (2 Cor 12:2-3), has the characteristics of ecstasy.

The experience of full union, and ecstasy if it is given, prepares the pilgrim for the *dark night of the spirit,* the last and narrowest tunnel of the spiritual journey toward wholeness in Christ. The dark night of the spirit is the eye of the needle through which no remaining vestiges of self-will may pass. It is the final stage of losing our "self" that it may be no longer we who live but Christ who lives in us (Gal 2:20). But such a losing is profoundly painful. It is indeed a dying, a crucifying, and is surrounded by the darkness of God's "absence" even as was the cross from which Jesus cried into the darkness, "My God, my God, why have you forsaken me?" (Mk 15:33-34). It is the anguish and darkness of losing our last grasp upon the handhold that keeps us from falling into the fiery abyss of Love. It is the darkness and despair of that moment of falling, between the final loss of our control and the awareness of the everlasting arms enfolding us in Love.

Once we have has relinquished all vestiges of self-control of the relationship with God and the world, we enter into the *transforming union* for which Jesus prayed: "I pray . . . for those who will believe in me . . . that they all may be one, *even as you, Father, are in me, and I in you,* that they also may be in us . . . that they may be one *even as we are one,* I in them and you in me, that they may become perfectly one" (Jn 17:20-23). Here is our ultimate conformity to the image of Christ—transforming oneness with God in Christ. But note especially the purpose or focus of this transforming union: "that they also may be in us, *so that the world may believe.* . . . that they may become perfectly one, *so that the world may know that you have sent me"* (vv. 21, 23). Wholeness in Christ, transforming union, is for the sake of others!

A Summary
This journey through the stages of awakening, purgation and illumination to union is accomplished in the vehicle of our personality, with its unique design of preference patterns and its ever-modulating psychological state. Such unique individual aspects of our jour-

ney call for a structured "guidance system" to keep the vehicle of our life on the route toward wholeness in Christ. The classical disciplines of the body of Christ provide such a guidance system. Individualized, privatized faith too easily allows us to settle comfortably within the limited confines of our preference pattern and psychological state. It is easier to keep God under control when our preferred patterns regulate our dynamics of behavior and relationship and where we have learned to accommodate to our psychological state. It is often on the less preferred side of our preference pattern, however, that God breaks in and upsets the little religious systems by which we try to keep God "safe" and under control.

God often disrupts our psychological state. Thus the community of faith becomes vital in our growth toward wholeness in Christ for others. The often disturbing, upsetting intrusions of others enable them to become agents of God's troubling grace in our pilgrimage. Our sisters and brothers in the faith also become God's agents of comfort, encouragement and support as we wrestle with the call to come out of the security of our incompleteness into the wholeness God has for us in Christ. It is in the community of faith that we find the support structures of the classical and personal spiritual disciplines, through which God conforms us to the wholeness of Christ for others.

Chapter 9

Classical Spiritual Disciplines

Gracious and loving God, I confess that the idea of "discipline" raises negative feelings and thoughts in me. Perhaps I think of discipline as punishment; it may raise dark shadows of long-forgotten and deeply buried abuse as a child. Perhaps I think of discipline as a heavy burden imposed upon me by some outside agency; it may call to mind such experiences from my past. I have difficulty thinking of discipline as a positive and creative dimension of my relationship with you. I especially have difficulty seeing spiritual disciplines as a means of your grace in my life. Can't you simply touch me at the points of my brokenness and incompleteness and make me well and whole? Help me, Lord, to receive what you have for me here. Help me to be willing to put my feet upon the narrow way of the disciplines that will bring me to complete freedom in your love.

---

*D*iscipline is not a popular term in our culture. Quaker writer Richard Foster's invitation to the "celebration of discipline"[1] is a radical call to a largely undisciplined and comfort-seeking culture. Our avoidance of discipline is anoother symptom of the pursuit of instant gratification which characterizes our culture. Instant fulfillment of needs and desires allows no time for the long and rigorous path of disciplines. Yet it is this path that brings true and lasting fulfillment, not the brief and fleeting appearances of fulfillment that disappear in the next moment.

While the avoidance of discipline characterizes much of our culture, the acceptance of disciplines can also be symptomatic of brokenness. There are those for whom disciplines become a rigid structure of life that allows no room for divine serendipities or graced interruptions of the disciplines. There are those for whom disciplines become such a fixed order of being and doing that the possibility of changes in the pattern becomes unthinkable. There are those for whom the disciplines become the total content of their relationship with God, and works righteousness the shape of their spirituality.

Somewhere between the extremes of avoidance of discipline and the imprisonment of discipline is the holistic practice of balanced spiritual disciplines which become a means of God's grace to shape us in the image of Christ for others. Paul seems to intimate this in his seemingly contradictory "Work out your own salvation . . . for God is at work in you" (Phil 2:12-13). Which is it, Paul—am I to work, or do I wait for God to do it? Paul's response would be "Yes!" You see, both sides of the equation are essential for balanced spiritual disciplines. If we destroy the paradox by opting for working out our own salvation, the disciplines by which we seek to do this work will become our prisons. If we destroy the paradox by opting for God to do everything, the absence of disciplines becomes a barrier that precludes God's opportunity to effect any consistent transformation in our lives. Holistic spiritual disciplines are acts of loving obedience that we offer to God steadily and consistently, to be used for whatever work God purposes to do in and through our lives.

Our tendency, however, is to destroy the tension of the paradox. We come down either on the side of do-it-yourself spirituality or on the side of waiting for God to do whatever God wants to do. This is why Paul says, "Work out your own salvation *with fear and trembling*, for God is at work in you." It is always difficult to maintain the delicate balance between working out our own salvation through spiritual disciplines and allowing God to work in us. It is so much easier to opt for one side against the other.

We also practice spiritual disciplines "with fear and trembling" because of the strong temptation to pervert the disciplines. We may exercise spiritual disciplines to attempt to win God's favor or to get God to do what we think ought to be done in our lives. We may practice the disciplines in the delusion that we are transforming ourselves into the image of Christ by our own efforts. We may engage in the disciplines to impress others with the seriousness of our spirituality, or simply to win acceptance by others.

The only pure motive for our spiritual disciplines is the motive of loving obedience to God. Only the motive of loving obedience will enable us to persist in the disciplines when the going gets rough, when nothing seems to be happening, when the old habits and attitudes of our brokenness seem unaffected by the disciplines that aim at their healing and transformation.

The very personalized spiritual disciplines to which God calls us are an integral part of the classical spiritual disciplines of the Christian tradition: prayer, spiritual reading, liturgy. These classical spiritual disciplines of the body of Christ form the scaffolding, the structure, the support network within which we then exercise the distinctive, personalized disciplines into which the Spirit of God leads each of us as we journey toward wholeness in Christ.

I have learned for myself, and have discovered in many of my brothers and sisters in Christ, that we don't always make the connection between the classical disciplines and our individual disciplines. While I was interested in resolving the brokenness and bondage of my own incompleteness, I thought this could be done by focused attention on those areas alone. I began to realize, however, that this was like trying to heal a disease while continuing to live in the habits and environment that cause the disease. While the treatment may be the correct one for the disease, without a change of the disease-causing environment or behavior there is little hope for healing.

We tend to think of the classical spiritual disciplines of the body of Christ as secondary or even optional to the "real" spirituality of our own private spiritual disciplines. But the classical disciplines serve to bring our lives into, and hold our lives in, God's environment for wholeness in Christ, so that the "treatment" of our individual disciplines can be fully effective.

Also, it is very difficult to maintain genuine personal disciplines without the scaffolding of the classical disciplines of the body of Christ. The classical disciplines give us the support structure within which our own spiritual disciplines become means of God's grace for the transformation of our being into the wholeness of Christ. Let us consider, then, some of the essential aspects of the classical disciplines.

Prayer

The consideration of *prayer* as a classical discipline of the Christian tradition[2] brings us up against the functional priorities of our culture. We tend to think of prayer as something we *do* in order to produce the results we believe are needed or, rather, to get God to produce the results. Go into any Christian bookstore and note the number of books devoted to techniques of prayer. We are interested in knowing what works and developing the skills that will ensure that our prayers are effective. As a result, our prayer tends to be a shopping list of things to be accomplished, an attempt to manipulate the symptoms of our lives without really entering into a deep, vital, transforming relationship with God in the midst of what we think we need (usually forgetting that "your Father knows what you need before you ask him" [Mt 6:8]) and in the midst of the symptoms of our lives (usually forgetting that "in everything God works together for good with those who love him" [Rom 8:28]).

Prayer, as a classical spiritual discipline, is primarily relational, not functional. Henri Nouwen, the modern Catholic spiritual writer, characterizes the nature of prayer succinctly:

> In a situation in which the world is threatened by annihilation, prayer does not mean much when we undertake it only as an attempt to influence God, or as a search for a spiritual fallout shelter, or as an offering of comfort in stress-filled times. . . . Prayer is the act by which we divest ourselves of all false belongings and become free to belong to God and God alone.[3]

What Nouwen points us to is the essence of prayer as a classical spiritual discipline—prayer as the reality of our relationship with God. This understanding of prayer, however, is most uncomfortable for us. As Nouwen adds:

> We want to move closer to God, the source and goal of our existence, but at the same time we realize that the closer we come to God the stronger will be his demand to let go of the many "safe" structures we have built around ourselves. Prayer is such a radical act because it requires us to criticize our whole way of being in the world, to lay down our old selves and accept our new self, which is Christ. . . . Prayer therefore is the act of dying to all that we consider to be our own and of being born to a new existence which is not of this world.[4]

This certainly puts our "shopping list" and "symptom manipulation" prayers in an entirely new light! These prayers may actually be our attempt to avoid such a radical relationship with God in the world, an attempt to keep God at arm's length and maintain control of our relationship with God on our terms. Prayer as a classical spiritual discipline draws us into God's involvement in the brokenness of the world on God's terms, not ours. (Are you beginning to see how the classical disciplines move us into a new environment, a new context for our healing?)

John saw into the depths of this reality in his vision of the opening of the seventh seal (Rev 8:1-5). The images of the angel, the altar, the coals and the incense relate to the incense offering on the Day of Atonement in the temple in Jerusalem. The incense offering was the liturgical act that began the daily office of temple worship. Usually, the priest selected to offer the incense offering was given a silver censer and about half a pound of incense. But on the Day of Atonement, the day on which the people of God were brought into full and perfect covenant relationship with God, the priest would be given a golden censer and as much incense as he could hold. The priest would then ascend the large sacrificial altar in the courtyard in front of the sanctuary. Upon this altar the sacrificial fire perpetually burned. The priest would scoop coals from the sacrificial fire into the censer and then descend from the altar. As he entered the sanctuary, he approached the Altar of Incense, the Golden Altar, which stood before the Holy of Holies, where God's presence was believed to dwell. He would place the coals on the altar and then drop the incense on the coals, and the smoke of the incense would rise into the presence of God in the Holy of Holies.

In John's vision, the angel is given much incense to mingle with the prayers of all the saints, another image that would have been familiar to Jewish Christians in the first century. The times of prayer in the synagogues were scheduled to coincide with the daily sacrifices at the temple in Jerusalem; prayer was associated with sacrifice. In John's vision, therefore, the prayers of the saints are mingled with the sacrificial fire of God's holiness in God's presence.

But then the vision introduces a new element. The angel scoops up the prayers of the saints, now incandescent from being purified by the sacrificial fire and inflamed in the presence of God, and casts them onto the earth. The result is thunder, voices, lightning and earthquake—all biblical images of the disruptive presence of God in the fallen world.[5]

John's vision is a powerful representation of the nature of prayer.

Prayer is the act by which the people of God become incorporated into the presence and action of God in the world. Prayer becomes a sacrificial offering of ourselves to God, to become agents of God's presence and action in the daily events and situations of our lives. How different this is from the idea of prayer as asking God to change our situation without any involvement on our part!

You probably realize that such prayer is most difficult to practice as an individual. We become so skilled at avoiding any real release of ourselves to God, any real sacrifice of our structures of security. This is undoubtedly why Jesus began the paradigm of prayer with the word *our*. We are taught to pray *"Our* Father," not *"My* Father," because there is an essentially corporate dimension to prayer. Corporate prayer lifts us out of the narrow, limited perspective of our individual needs and desires and provides us with the broader, deeper vision of vital relationship with and sacrificial response to God in the midst of our life and world.

This is why we should, as individuals and communities of faith, make use of the prayers of the church that have come down to us from the past. This is why, as individuals and communities of faith, we should pray the psalter. This is the essence of the classical spiritual discipline of prayer: not our private, individualized prayers, but immersing ourselves in the deep, sacrificial prayers of the saints through which the church through the ages has offered itself to be the body of Christ in the world. Unless our individual prayer life exists within the greater support structure of the prayers of the saints, it will tend to become very narrow, individualized and privatized, and we will shy away from yielding control of our existence for God's purposes in our world.

Paul's Vision of Prayer
Paul develops this theme in his prayer instructions to the body of Christ at Philippi (Phil 4:4-7).[6] He begins by reminding the Philippians to rejoice in the Lord, thus setting the only proper context for

true prayer: our vital relationship with God in Jesus Christ. Paul heightens this emphasis when he adds, "Let everyone know your life is being lived in another structure of being, one in which the Lord is constantly a vital presence."[7]

We must remember that Paul is writing to a Christian community, not to an individual. These instructions on prayer are for the community first, the individual members second. It is within the body of Christ that the reality of the new order of being in Christ is maintained and nurtured as the ruling perspective for life and activity. The community of faith is the primary and essential means by which individual believers are nurtured to understand and live their lives as citizens of God's New Jerusalem in the midst of a fallen-Babylon world.

Paul next reminds the Christian community in Philippi not to be "anxious." The term is descriptive of a mode of existence characterized by attempting to control one's life. This kind of anxiety arises whenever we attempt to impose and maintain our own manipulative control upon the world, whenever we attempt to squeeze the world into our own mold. The world, of course, resists our control and threatens the entire structure of protection and security we have so carefully constructed around our lives. How can we be liberated from such a mode of existence?

Paul tells the Philippians that such liberation comes when "in everything, by prayer and supplication with thanksgiving, [we] make [our] requests known to God" (v. 6 RSV). Notice the list that precedes our requests. "In everything" denotes an established posture of relationship with God that becomes the context within which we experience all the events and relationships of our lives. "By prayer" indicates the active exercise of this established relationship as the initial response to each event and relationship. "Supplication" implies an awareness of our inability to meet the events and relationships of our lives in our own strength or by our own resources. "With thanksgiving" reveals a posture of being that is yielded and responsive to God's presence and purpose in every event and relationship. Paul intimates that only when our lives take this kind of posture toward God are we able to make proper requests of God.

This kind of corporate prayer, which nurtures and supports the same kind of individual prayer, is the paradigm of the classical spiritual discipline of prayer. When our prayers, corporate and individual, conform to this model, Paul tells us that "the peace of God, which passes all understanding, will keep [our] hearts and [our] minds in Christ Jesus" (v. 7 RSV). God's *shalom* (peace) is the order of life in relationship with God in which true wholeness and fulfillment is experienced. This is not an escapist kind of peace; it exists in the midst of events and relationships that threaten to undo us. Thus it "passes all understanding." This peace has produced saints and martyrs through whom the destructive, dehumanizing dynamics of the world have been shaken and undone in age after age. This is the essence of the classical spiritual discipline of prayer, and the context within which we offer to God our individual spiritual disciplines.

Spiritual Reading

The classical spiritual discipline of spiritual reading[8] brings us into conflict with the informational priorities of our culture. Our age has been called the information age, and the advent of personal computers coupled with modems has served to expand almost infinitely the amount of information available to us and required for effective performance in the world. Information has become power. The person or group possessing the best information is in a position to control their world of activity and interest.

But this "controlling" aspect of our approach to information becomes a debilitating bondage when we approach spiritual reading. Spiritual reading is the discipline of openness to encounter God through the writings of the mothers and fathers of the church, beginning with the Scriptures. In spiritual reading the text becomes a means of grace through which we encounter the God who has spoken us forth into being and who continues to speak to us to shape us in the image of Christ for others. In brief, the text opens us to God's control of our lives for God's purposes. This is a radical reversal of the dynamics of an informational culture in which our possession and use of information enables us to impose our purposes upon the world of our activities.

Unfortunately, we have been trained to be informational readers, not spiritual readers. When we do informational reading, we exercise almost total and complete control over the text. We usually select the material we are going to read. We read the text with our own agenda already in place, knowing in advance what we expect to receive, what problems we want the text to solve for us. We read the text analytically, viewing it as an object over which we as subject exercise our control, to ensure that it conforms more or less comfortably to our desires and purposes. We read the text as rapidly as possible, to amass as much information as we can in as little time as possible. (Have you ever caught yourself marking your place and looking ahead to see how much was left?) The final goal of informational reading is our mastery of the text for the fulfillment of our purposes.

Spiritual or *formational* reading is the exact opposite of informational reading. Spiritual reading is entered into best, perhaps, when the text is chosen for us—for instance, by the use of a lectionary. This way we begin by yielding control to someone or something outside of our agenda. This facilitates one of the primary purposes of spiritual reading—to allow the text to have control over us and become a place of encounter with God. Instead of the text being an object controlled by us, the text becomes the subject; we, in turn, become the "object" addressed by God through the text.

Instead of coming to the text with our agenda, we come in a posture of openness to God's agenda. We read attentively, seeking not to cover as much as possible as quickly as possible but to plumb the depths of the text so that the text may plumb the depths of our being and doing. Rather than an analytical approach, we take a contemplative posture that is open to ambiguity and mystery. The final goal of spiritual reading is to be mastered by God for the fulfillment of God's purposes in us and through us.[9]

By this contrast I do not intend to suggest that informational reading is "bad" and formational reading is "good." Each has its proper place. The difficulty arises from the fact that we are so deeply conditioned by informational reading that it tends to be the mode by which we approach all reading. The deeply ingrained habits of informational reading tend to take over whenever we open a book. We do not naturally engage in formational reading. We need to be alert to this fact if we are going to engage in spiritual reading.

Lectio Divina

The discipline of spiritual reading finds its classical expression in what is known as *lectio divina.*[10] Lectio is a posture of approach and a means of encounter with a text that enables the text to become a place of transforming encounter with God. We will see, as we explore each component of lectio divina, that one of its great strengths is its holistic interplay between the sensing-intuitive and thinking-feeling aspects of our preference patterns. It is an excellent discipline of holistic spirituality. Table 4, on the next page, provides an overview of lectio divina.

The classical form of lectio divina has four components: *lectio, meditatio, oratio* and *contemplatio.* Before we explore these, however, we should note that introducing and concluding components need to be added for us—components that enable lectio to be effective for persons shaped by an informational culture such as ours. The introductory element is *silencio,* and the concluding element is *incarnatio.*[11]

Silencio is our preparation for spiritual reading. Shaped as we are

Table 4. Lectio Divina

Silencio	Preparation for spiritual reading
	Inner shift from control to receptivity
	from information to formation
	from observation to obedience
Lectio	Reading/receiving
	Nurtures "sensing" dynamic
Meditatio	Processing
	Nurtures "thinking" dynamic
Oratio	Response to God from the heart
	Nurtures "feeling" dynamic
Contemplatio	Yielding and waiting upon God
	Nurtures "intuitive" dynamic
Incarnatio	Living out the text

by an informational culture, trained to approach a text as the ones who are in control of the text, we need to take time, at the beginning of the process of spiritual reading, to engage in an deep internal shift in the posture of our being.

One of John Wesley's guidelines for reading the Bible deals pointedly with this shift. Wesley suggests that we come to the text "with a single eye, to know the whole will of God, and a fixed resolution to do it."[12] The first half of Wesley's guideline, if left by itself, can be totally informational. We can honestly and sincerely desire to know the whole will of God for our lives, but then set it alongside our own set of purposes so that we can choose what we think is the best. The second half of Wesley's guideline introduces the shift required in the deep inner posture of our being. It is a shift of the control of the process from ourselves to God. It is a deep commitment of our being to God's purposes, even before we know what those purposes may be.

Lectio, the first step in the classical discipline of spiritual reading,

114   *Invitation to a Journey* ■

is simply the process of reading the text. This activity nurtures the
sensing side of our temperament. We hold the book in our hands
and feel its texture. Our eyes follow the words on the page. If we
make it a practice to read aloud, our ears hear the words and our
tongues "taste" them. We might even use incense to engage our
sense of smell in the process of taking the text into our being. We
read expectantly, hungry to hear what God has to say to us, recep-
tive to whatever God says and willing to respond in loving obedience to whatever we receive. Lectio might be likened to taking
food into our mouths, receiving the nourishment our lives need
from God.

Meditatio is the activity of processing what we have received in
lectio, and flows naturally from our reading. If lectio is viewed as
receiving food, meditatio is the process of "chewing" it. This activity
nurtures the thinking side of our temperament. In meditatio we
seek understanding and comprehension of the text. We may need
to engage in study of the passage, look up unfamiliar terms or
phrases, research background information. In all of this activity,
however, we never lose sight of the fact that we are seeking to hear
what God is saying to us in the text. And not simply to hear ("to
know the whole will of God") but to respond ("a fixed intent to do
it").

Oratio is our response to God on the basis of what we have read
and encountered, and flows naturally from meditatio. At this point
we enter into personal dialogue with God. This activity nurtures
the feeling side of our temperament. We share with God the feelings the text has aroused in us, feelings such as love, joy, sorrow,
anger, repentance, desire, need, conviction, consecration. We pour
out our heart to God in complete openness and honesty, especially
as the text has probed aspects of our being and doing in the midst
of various issues and relationships.

At the close of oratio, *contemplatio* moves us into a posture of
released waiting on God for whatever God wants to do in us, with

us, through us. This activity nurtures the intuitive side of our temperament. It is a posture of yieldedness to God. Some translations of the psalm capture it well: "Truly I have set my soul in silence and in peace, like a weaned child at its mother's breast" (Ps 131:2).[13] The unweaned child is at its mother's breast for what it wants—milk. The weaned child, however, is content to rest in its loving mother's arms and receive whatever she desires to give. Contemplatio is the posture of the weaned child. We abandon ourselves to God and to whatever God wants to do with us.

To these four steps of lectio divina we must add a concluding step, *incarnatio*. The whole focus of spiritual reading is to encounter God in ways that enable God to transform our being and doing in the world. Again, Wesley puts it well: "Whatever light you then receive should be used to the uttermost, and that immediately. Let there be no delay. Whatever you resolve begin to execute the first moment you can."[14] This step brings us full circle to what we do in silencio. There we placed ourselves before the text to seek the whole will of God with "a fixed resolution to do it." Incarnatio is the fulfillment of that resolution.

The classical spiritual discipline of spiritual reading is one of the most vital in our growth toward wholeness in the image of Christ for others. Out of the discipline of spiritual reading come many of the highly individualized and personal disciplines which God calls us to offer as means of transforming grace.

Liturgy

This somewhat daunting term literally means "the work of the people." It has mistakenly come to be used almost exclusively for elaborate patterns of worship and celebration. Liturgy certainly includes such high times of community activity, but it also includes the simple orders of worship, the spontaneous celebrations of God, our personal structures of daily devotion and all the patterns of activity by which we seek to enter into deeper relationship with God, corporate relationship with one another and faithful response to God in our daily lives.

If prayer and spiritual reading are the means by which we are awakened to the deeper realities of life in Christ and called into the discipleship of a new order of being in Christ, then liturgy is the diverse structure of behaviors that serve to nurture us in that new order of being.

Throughout our lives we have been consciously and unconsciously shaped by the habits of the old order of being, which has held us in dehumanizing bondage. Our attitudes, our perspectives, our ways of relating to others, our methods of responding to the circumstances of the world around us, our self-image, even our understanding of God have all been shaped by the destructive values and dehumanizing structures of the world's brokenness. Daily those values have been and are still the atmosphere in which we live. Daily those structures set limits upon our actions. The media, the entertainment world, the advertising industry all serve to maintain, reinforce and extend the destructive value systems of our non-Christian culture. Political, economic and social structures exert tremendous pressure upon the individual to conform to the prevailing patterns of perception and behavior.

To be followers of Christ is to be persons whose lives, individually and corporately, are lived by a set of values radically different from those of the broken world, persons whose behaviors are shaped by the structures of a different order of being—the kingdom of God. To be empowered to live such lives of radical dissonance in the world, lives that mediate the transforming and healing grace of God to the brokenness of the world, the people of God need individual and corporate support structures that consistently nurture them in the values of God's new order of being in Christ and provide behavior patterns that enable them to live as faithful citizens of God's New Jerusalem. In the broader sense of the term, liturgy is such a support structure.

Liturgy consists of the corporate and individual patterns of devotion, worship, fellowship and obedience that enable us increasingly to manifest in the world God's kingdom of love, forgiveness, reconciliation, cleansing, healing and holiness. This is why Kenneth Leech affirms:

> The liturgy is thus a deeply subversive act, a spiritual force working within the fallen world to undermine it and renew it. . . . To take part in the Christian liturgy is to take on one's role in a new kingdom: one that "shall have no end." It is the political act of all time and is therefore potentially seditious within the secular politics of a specific time and place. . . . Liturgy should be an act of festivity, of joy, of liberation, an act in which the powers of the age to come are celebrated in anticipation.[15]

The Components of Liturgy

With this understanding of liturgy, let us now consider briefly some specific elements of liturgy. Two of them—prayer and spiritual healing—we have already looked at in some depth. But there are others that round out the classical discipline of liturgy: worship, daily office, study, fasting and retreat.

Worship, whether corporate or individual (and there needs to be both in our liturgical discipline) is the practice of regularly seeking to bring the complete focus of our being upon God. It is the discipline of returning to the true center of our individual and corporate existence as God's people. The pressures of life and the assaults of the fallen world constantly blur our focus and tend to shift us away from our center in God. Worship is the means by which we recover our focus and return to our center. The quality and consistency of our worship will determine how well we are able to live Christ-centered lives in the world.

Daily office is regular and consistent daily behaviors that remind us whose we are and renew us in our discipleship. These may be as elaborate and complex as monastic hours of personal and corporate prayer or as simple as a daily time of personal devotion. A daily office might include such elements as personal quiet time with God (or several such times during the day—morning, midday, evening or a combination); prayers before meals; moments of prayer dispersed through the day at planned points; gathering with others daily for worship, prayer, Bible study, Christian fellowship. Whatever the form of our daily office, we need such a discipline if we are to live our lives in a growing experience of the wholeness of Christ and in increasing faithfulness as God's persons for others.

Study is essential for the Christian's growth toward wholeness in Christ for the sake of others. Without disciplined growth in our knowledge and experience of God, ourselves, others and the world around us, we are handicapped in our growth toward wholeness in Christ and our ability to be God's person for others. The discipline of individual and corporate study keeps us aware of our growth needs, alert to the vital issues of the world around us and sensitized to what God is doing to grow us up into Christ and call us forth to be agents of grace in the midst of the world's issues. With the discipline of study, however, we must be alert to the temptation to enter into the discipline as a means to help us exert greater control over our lives, the lives of others and the problems of the world. The liturgy of study, as with all the elements of liturgy, is a means of offering ourselves to God, willing for God to do with us as God chooses.

Fasting involves far more than abstaining from food, although such abstention is certainly called for in the midst of a gluttonous and overweight culture.[16] The essence of fasting is the separation of ourselves from something in order to offer ourselves in greater measure to God. While what we fast from may be detrimental to our life or our relationship with God, generally the point of fasting is to separate ourselves temporarily (as in the case of food) or permanently (as in a vow of celibacy) from something that is normally a good and proper part of human life.

One of the main purposes of fasting is to wean us from our dependence upon God's gifts and enable us to become dependent upon God alone. We have a powerful tendency to grasp for ourselves the gifts God gives for the meeting of life's needs. We constantly succumb to the temptation to become dependent on these things for our well-being and wholeness. Whenever our grasp of something God has given for our sustenance and well-being becomes a destructive bondage of dependence—an idol—a discipline of fasting is needed.

Retreat is the discipline of setting apart a time, individually or corporately, to step aside from the normal flow of life and give God our full and undivided attention. While the disciplines of prayer, spiritual reading, worship, daily office, study and fasting all serve as means to clarify the focus of our life in Christ and keep us centered as citizens of God's new order of being, we also need special times in which we allow God to help us reevaluate the whole structure of our life in Christ. We need to stand aside from our discipleship so as to be able to see more clearly the direction in which we are going and the course corrections God would have us make. It is possible for the practice of the classical disciplines itself to become a subtle form of works righteousness in which we come to think that by our faithful exercise of the disciplines we are *transforming ourselves* into the image of Christ. We need to take times to stand aside and allow God to show us what we are doing and what we ought to be doing.

In conclusion, we must remember that these classical disciplines of the Christian tradition are the support structure within which we offer the very personalized disciplines through which God will work to bring our brokenness into wholeness, our deadness into life and our bondage into freedom. It is to the personal disciplines that we now turn.

Chapter 10

The Nature of the Spiritual Disciplines

*O God, the consideration of the classical spiritual disciplines has
awakened me to the radical nature of being a disciple of
Jesus. I have seen so many aspects of my practice of Christianity
that have simply been my own form of works righteousness.
I have seen many areas of my discipleship that need to be
reconsidered. I have been challenged to undertake frighteningly new
disciplines and to begin to walk in unknown paths with you.
If the classical disciplines are so challenging, what do the personal
disciplines hold for me? Help me to be open and available
to you, to place my life at your disposal, that you may fulfill your
purposes in me and through me.*

*T*he classical spiritual disciplines support and nurture us in the
healing perspectives and holistic behaviors of God's realm of wholeness in Christ. They also call us to the more personal disciplines that
deal with the unique shape of our personal brokenness. If we are to
grow toward wholeness in the image of Christ for the sake of others,
we need to understand the nature of personal spiritual disciplines,
those very individual acts of loving obedience offered for God's use
to transform our unlikeness to Christ into wholeness in Christ.

In the midst of the well-known eighth chapter of Romans, there is a section that does not receive the attention it should. This section is puzzling at first reading, but closer scrutiny discloses the nature of spiritual disciplines and reveals how we work and how God works to transform our deadness into life, our brokenness into wholeness, our bondage into freedom in Christ.

Paul makes a very strange statement in Romans 8:10. He begins, "If Christ is in you." This sets the context of those whom he is addressing. He is addressing persons in whom Christ dwells; obviously, he is speaking to Christians. He is speaking to born-again Christians, the regenerated, the redeemed, saved persons, or whatever term you apply to persons who know, in some way, the presence of the risen Christ in their lives, not as a theological theory but as an experiential reality.

Paul then says there are two conditions that prevail "if Christ is in you": "your body is dead because of sin, yet your spirit is alive because of righteousness." We don't have too much difficulty with the latter statement, that our spirits are alive because of righteousness. It is my sincere hope that you are reading this book because at some point in your life you have had an encounter with the risen Lord and in response to that encounter your spirit came alive because of the new right relationship with God (or righteousness) that had been graced to you in Jesus Christ. This experience takes as many different forms as there are people who experience it. For some it is a radical, 180-degree conversion experience. For others it is a slower, gradual, dawning consciousness of Christ's presence that graces to them new life in relationship to God. If your spirit has come alive in this way, you won't have too much difficulty understanding what Paul means when he says, "If Christ is in you . . . your spirit is alive because of righteousness."

But what on earth does Paul mean when he says that if Christ is in us, our bodies are dead because of sin? Here is the mystery! One of the common ways to cut through the difficulty of this statement is simply to say that Paul means our physical beings are going to die because of the Fall. But Paul does not say our bodies *will die* because of sin; he says our bodies *are dead* because of sin.

In the Greek, Paul does not even use the verb denoting "being." The absence of the verb meaning "to be" is a grammatical form often employed in the Greek language to indicate an existing state of being. Paul is emphasizing a present reality to his readers: their bodies are presently "dead" because of sin. Now the Romans may have been worshiping in the catacombs, but they were not buried there yet. They were as alive as you and I are. What, then, does Paul mean when he says, "Your body is dead because of sin," even at the same time that "your spirit is alive because of righteousness"?

The Dead Body

When I began wrestling with this a few years ago, one of the first things I did was to see how Paul uses this word *body*, because it appears that he is talking about something other than physical existence. I discovered that Paul uses the term *body* (Greek *sōma*) in three different ways. First, he does use the word for physical existence. For instance, elsewhere in Romans Paul speaks of people who dishonor their bodies by homosexual unions (1:24-27), of Abraham, who did not lose faith in God's promise of an heir even though his body was aged (4:19-21) and of how our physical bodies consist of many members (12:4). Second, Paul also uses *body* to refer to a corporate entity. This is especially the case when he speaks of the Christian community as the body of Christ. For instance, again in Romans, Paul indicates that through incorporation into the body of Christ, Jewish believers stand in a radically new relationship to the law of Moses—it no longer rules them, but Christ does (7:1-4)— and that all believers make up one body in Christ (12:5). Whenever Paul uses *body* in either of these two ways, the context makes it clear which use he intends.

But then I discovered that Paul uses *body* a third way that does not fit the first two. One of these uses is in Romans 6:6. There Paul is speaking to the Romans (and to us) about what had taken place when they were baptized into Christ (6:1-5). Then, in 6:6, he says, "We know that our old self was crucified with him so that the body of sin might be made inoperative,[1] that we might no longer be enslaved to sin." Body of sin? What is this body of sin?

In Romans 5, Paul has a long discourse on the relationship between sin and death. I suspect that there may be some legitimacy in proposing that the "body of sin" in 6:6 is in some way equivalent to that "body of death," or "dead body," that Paul speaks about in Romans 8:10.

It is important to notice one thing Paul says about this "body of sin." Even though our old being was crucified with Christ, it was so that the body of sin *might* be made inoperative. Not that it has been, as something already accomplished, not that it automatically will be in the future, but that it *might* be.

There is a potentiality here because of what we have experienced through our baptism into Christ. Paul's language implies that there is something of this "body of sin" still present in our lives, although we need no longer be held in bondage by it. Whatever the "body of sin" might be, Paul asserts that God has done something in Christ that, through our baptism into Christ, makes it possible for us to be liberated from bondage to the "body of sin."

Then, in the seventh chapter of Romans, Paul gives us a much clearer picture of what he is talking about. Paul speaks of an experience that is part of our own pilgrimage: "I do not understand my own actions. For I do not do what I want, but I do the very thing I hate" (v. 15). Three verses later he adds, "I can will what is right, but I cannot do it. For I do not do the good I want, but the evil I do not want is what I do" (vv. 18-19). He continues, "When I want to do right, evil lies close at hand" (v. 21). Then Paul makes a most significant statement, one that is vital for our understanding of the reality he is conveying. He affirms, "I delight in the law of God in my inmost being" (v. 22).

There have been many in my own Wesleyan tradition, and particularly in its Holiness branch, who have explained Romans 7 as describing Paul before he became a Christian. I do not believe this is possible in light of 7:22. When, in the midst of this repeated litany of doing the evil he does not want to do and failing to do the good he wants, Paul says, "I delight in the law of God in my inmost being," it sounds very similar to how John Wesley describes a person who is entirely sanctified. Wesley speaks of how "the will is entirely subject to the will of God and the affections wholly fixed on him. Now what motive can remain sufficient to induce such a person to a transgression of the law?"[2] Does not this describe a person who delights in the law of God in the inner being?

Wesley adds that such persons, through human weakness, may unintentionally speak or do things that are "condemned by the perfect law."[3] Albert Outler, the leading twentieth-century authority on Wesley, notes that this is "another version of Wesley's distinction between deliberate and undeliberate sins; one who is 'perfect' does not sin *deliberately.*"[4] Wesley has a bit of difficulty here linguistically, because he doesn't want to call such behavior "sin" as Paul does; Wesley calls it "mistakes" or "omissions." But the key for Wesley is the same as for Paul. For Wesley, sin is restricted to *voluntary* transgressions of the will of God, and mistakes and omissions are *involuntary* transgressions.

While Paul isn't being quite as linguistically sophisticated as Wesley, he is saying the same thing. What he does, he is not willing to do; these acts are involuntary transgressions of the will of God. For he repeatedly indicates that the evil he does is not what he wants to do—it is not deliberate; instead, he wants to do good, for he delights in the law of God in his inmost being. Paul says, "I will to do what is right" (v. 18). That is his will, that is his purpose, that is his desire, yet Paul finds that there is another law at work, making him a captive to the law of sin that dwells in his members (v. 23).

And then comes Paul's piercing cry, "Wretched man that I am!

Who will deliver me from *this body of death?"* (v. 24). There's that dead body again! But now we have a much better idea of what Paul is talking about. The "dead body" has something to do with doing evil when we desire to do good—even when we delight in the law of God in our inmost being.

I am sure this experience has been part of your own pilgrimage in Christ: the good you want to do, you do not do, while the evil you do not want to do is what you do.

The History of Our Dead Body

What is Paul dealing with? Before your spirit came alive because of righteousness, this is what you looked like:

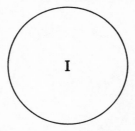

Figure 1

Before we allowed Jesus to exercise any degree of lordship, *we* were the lord of our lives. From the center of our being to the outermost fringes, *we* were lord. Our will, our desire, our interest, our agenda, our program, our plan, our purpose, our wants, our needs regulated our existence. We were in control of our own being, and under our own control we developed a whole structure of habits, attitudes, perspectives, dynamics of relationship, ways of reacting and responding to the world around us.

We developed, you might say, a "body of being" made up of this complex network of habits and attitudes. The entire network was constructed under our own lordship. The parts of the network were geared to fulfilling our own purposes so that we could inflict our

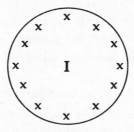

Figure 2

own will upon the world around us and regulate that world as much
as possible for our own purposes and desires.

Then, at some point, by God's grace our spirit came alive because
of righteousness.

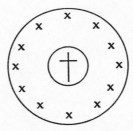

Figure 3

At some point in our life we were encountered by the risen Christ
and made a response that brought us into the faith pilgrimage. But
what about the network of habits, attitudes and perspectives relating to the world? It is still there!

I suspect you may have experienced something like the kind of
experience I once heard a young man describe. He had had one of
those radical, 180-degree conversion experiences, and for about
three weeks or so he sort of floated along in a third heaven, his feet
hardly touching the ground in the euphoria of that experience of
joy and release as his spirit came alive in Christ. But, he said,
one day he woke up and discovered that there were whole areas of

his life that had never even heard of Jesus Christ. He was discovering the reality of what Paul speaks of as the "dead body." Yes, his spirit was alive because of righteousness. There was no doubt about that in his life, but he was beginning to realize the reality of Romans 7.

Here is the reality of this "dead body." Those old harmful habits, those deeply ingrained imprisoning attitudes, those troubling and damaging perspectives, those destructive ways of relating to others, those unhealthy modes of reacting and responding to the world go way down deep into our being. This is what Paul is talking about when he says that our body is dead because of sin.

Fortunately, Paul doesn't stop with his cry, "Who will deliver me from this body of death?" He continues, "Thanks be to God through Jesus Christ our Lord" (Rom 7:25). There is the promise of deliverance from the dead body. This body of sin *can* be made inoperative. But then Paul adds, "So then, I of myself serve the law of God with my inmost being,[5] but with my flesh I serve the law of sin. There is, therefore, now no condemnation for those who are in Christ Jesus. For the law of the spirit of life in Christ Jesus has set me free from the law of sin and death" (7:25—8:2).

What I hear Paul saying is that this experience of the "dead body" is a normal part of our Christian pilgrimage. Let me clarify: I am not saying that it is *normative*. We will see that Paul takes us beyond this. But the experience of Romans 7—the reality of the "dead body," those old harmful habits, deeply ingrained attitudes, troubling perspectives, destructive ways of relating to others, unhealthy modes of reacting and responding to the world—is a normal part of our Christian pilgrimage. Many Christians have difficulty with this reality. We tend to think that if all of our old nature has not been done away with in conversion or sanctification, then we really have not become Christian. Paul does not support this: "If Christ is in you, your body is dead because of sin, yet your spirit is alive because of righteousness."

Life out of Death

Paul does not leave us in this condition. He continues, "If the Spirit of the One who raised Jesus from the dead dwells in you, the One who raised Christ Jesus from the dead will make alive your dead body[6] also through the Spirit which dwells in you" (8:11). Notice the change in terms: in 8:10 it was "If Christ is in you"; here it is "If the Spirit of the One who raised Christ Jesus from the dead dwells in you," and Paul states it twice to further emphasize God as the One who brings life out of death.

Here is the great work of God in the process of spiritual formation. God is at work in the areas of our deadness to transform them into life in the image of Christ. This is the essential nature of our pilgrimage. Here is where God is working to conform each of us to the image of Christ for the sake of others. God's work is unique in each person, because none of us has exactly the same configuration of the dead body. Our "dead body," that complex structure of harmful habits, deeply ingrained attitudes, troubling perspectives, destructive ways of relating to others, unhealthy modes of reacting and responding to the world, is very individual. We may share some of the same general forms of deadness, but the nature of our particular deadness is always uniquely shaped to us. So Paul tells us that although this condition (spirit alive because of righteousness, body dead because of sin) is a normal part of Christian experience, it is also the base from which God works to move us toward wholeness in Christ.

Our Response

Paul then discusses two possible responses to our condition. He first tells us, "We are not debtors to the flesh, to live according to the flesh, for if you continue to live according to the flesh, you are about to die"[7] (8:12-13). What I hear Paul saying is, "If you continue to allow the dynamics of your deadness to shape your behavior, you will make shipwreck of your faith." Death, for Paul, is the condition of the unredeemed person: "Once you were dead in the trespasses and sins in which you once walked" (Eph 2:1; see also Col 2:13). For those whose spirits have come alive (Rom 8:10) to continue to allow the "dead body" to rule their lives is to gradually slip back into the deadness out of which they were called to life.

But Paul gives us a second option, "If, by the Spirit, you put to death the deeds of the body, you will live" (8:13). Here is where Paul puts his finger on the dynamics of that very personalized set of spiritual disciplines by which God raises our deadness into life, our brokenness into wholeness, and conforms us to the image of Christ for others.

I would suggest that you take one of the elements of your "dead body" as an illustration for yourself as you read on. It may be a harmful habit. It may be a disruptive attitude. It may be a destructive relationship. You know what it is. When you are completely honest with yourself, you know at least one area of your life where your "body" is dead because of sin. You know of at least one thing in your life that is not in harmony with God's purpose for your wholeness in the image of Christ. Focus on that. Let that be your example as we work through what Paul is saying here.

Let's use our illustration of our condition if Christ is in us, and pull out that element you have chosen to focus upon (see figure 4).

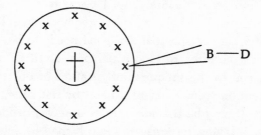

Figure 4

This element is that brokenness within you where something of your being has been distorted away from the image of Christ. This "dead body" (B) results in a certain behavior pattern—deeds (D). The "body" of our being (B) and our doing or deeds (D) are inseparably linked, and Paul always keeps them together in his writings.

Paul says, "If by the Spirit . . ." Do you remember what Jesus said about one of the roles of the Holy Spirit? "When the Spirit comes, he will convict the world of sin" (Jn 16:8). We discussed in chapter three how the process of being conformed to the image of Christ takes place at those points where we are *not* conformed. God's approach, God's touch, is at the points of our unlikeness to Christ—our "dead body." Here is where the Spirit probes us.

The Spirit usually probes us at the point of some behavior pattern, some deed of our "dead body." That behavior pattern (D) is the outward manifestation, in the way we conduct our life in the world with others, of the deadness of the body of our being (B) from which that behavior pattern flows. Paul says that when the Spirit awakens us, alerts us to that kind of dynamic in our life, if we put to death the deeds of the "dead body" we will live.

I hear Paul calling us to begin to offer to God a behavior that is patterned on the image of Christ—a spiritual discipline. Usually it is not too hard for us to figure out the nature of such a discipline. I have discovered that when God's Spirit probes one of the areas of my deadness, not only do I begin to see that portion of my own "dead body" but, at the same time, I begin to understand what wholeness in Christ looks like, at least to some degree. I have some initial idea of what the spiritual discipline needs to be. This is the point at which we offer to God a personal spiritual discipline, a discipline shaped to the unique configuration of our deadness. It may be abstention from a harmful habit or the substitution of a healthy habit. It may be the adoption of a new attitude by an act of our will as a loving response to God. It may be severing a destructive relationship, or it may be structuring a whole new way of continuing that relationship. It may be a different way of responding to certain situations.

The Essence of Spiritual Disciplines

Let me clarify the nature of a spiritual discipline, because here our cultural shaping distorts our understanding. We tend to think of spiritual disciplines as something that we are doing to transform ourselves, to make alive our "dead body." Go back a couple of verses in Romans. It is only the One who raised Christ Jesus from the dead who can bring life out of deadness. We cannot do it. There is nothing that you or I can do to change the nature of our dead body. That is God's realm. What we *can* do is to offer to God the spiritual discipline that God stirs within us by the Spirit.

If we're thinking we are changing ourselves by offering the spiritual discipline, we are deluding ourselves. We may be able to keep up that discipline for a week, a month, several months, but sooner or later we're going to "fall off the wagon" and discover that the old dead body is just as alive as it ever was (if I may mix my metaphors). It is still there; it hasn't changed; all those weeks and months of disciplines haven't done a thing to transform that deadness into life in Christ's image. If anything, the deadness seems even stronger, because it has been fasting so long. So we go on a gorging binge. Whatever that brokenness is, we find ourselves indulging horribly in it. Then guilt and remorse begin to build up, and we get back "on the wagon," pick up the discipline, grab our bootstraps and try to pull ourselves back up.

This is not a spiritual discipline. If you have had that rollercoaster experience—trying to maintain the discipline, falling off, starting it again and falling off, starting it again and falling off—it may be because you've not been offering God a genuine discipline. You may have been trying a do-it-yourself operation, a form of works righteousness.

A genuine spiritual discipline is a discipline of loving obedience offered to God with no strings attached. We put no conditions on it. We put no time limits on it. We add no expectation of how we want God to change us through it. We simply offer the discipline to God, and keep on offering it for as long as God wants us to keep on.

This is not easy! Genuine spiritual disciplines are hard work. So we need our brothers and sisters in Christ to support us, to hold us in their care, to bear the burden with us. I believe this is what James is talking about when he says, "Confess your sins to one another" (Jas 5:16). This is not some sort of spiritual exhibitionism. It is saying to a group of faithful, trusted sisters and brothers in Christ, "Here is the area of my deadness where the Spirit of God is calling me to faithful obedience, and I need your help. Hold me accountable for this discipline until the work God wants to do in me through it is done." This is also what Paul is saying when he exhorts us to "bear one another's burdens, and thus fulfill the law of Christ" (Gal 6:2).

The various Twelve-Step programs that have proliferated in recent years have grasped the significance of this essential spiritual principle. Members of such groups always stand ready to go to a sister or brother who is weakening under the assault of the temptation to succumb to brokenness. They will stay with them, encourage them, support them and see them through until they win the victory consistently. This is a vital essential of holistic spirituality that the church has lost.

In some of the more superficial disciplines we may be able to work it out—just us and the Lord. But let me tell you if you haven't discovered this already, when God begins to work with the deep-down brokenness of your life, there is no way you can do it by yourself. No way!

Why? Because when you start offering the spiritual discipline, you discover there is warfare inside you. That dead body of your being wants to continue to express itself in the old, destructive behaviors, and through the discipline you are doing the opposite; you have got a war going on. This is what Paul is talking about when he says, "The desires of the flesh are against the Spirit and the desires of the Spirit are against the flesh" (Gal 5:17). He is not talking about Christians and non-Christians; he is talking about Christian experience. Paul is writing in the context of walking by the Spirit (Gal 5:16), and he is saying that when you start walking by the Spirit a war breaks out in your life: the flesh will war against the Spirit, and the Spirit will war against the flesh.

And that is exactly what happens. We start offering a discipline and the dead body of our being starts saying, "No! No! No! No! I want to behave in the old way!" And the Spirit is saying,"Yes! Yes! Yes! Yes! Pursue this new behavior!"

Here we begin to see something of the depths of our spiritual disciplines. Here is where we begin our dying to self, the taking up of our cross. I don't know about you, but I know that when that warfare gets strong I can become amazingly subtle; I can rationalize beautifully a million reasons it's perfectly okay to go back to the old behaviors, the old deadness. And it makes perfectly logical, rational sense. It can even seem pious, except that I know deep down in my heart that it isn't. This is why I need others who will keep on saying, "Come on, Bob, quit kidding yourself, hang in there, push on, keep on offering the discipline."

When we continue to offer the discipline, that discipline becomes a means of grace through which God works and moves to transform that dead portion of our body into life in the image of Christ. One morning you wake up and discover, often to your amazement, that the discipline is no longer a discipline; it is now the natural outflow of a being that has been raised to new life in Christ—that the Spirit of the One who raised Christ Jesus from the dead, the Spirit who also dwells in you, has made alive your dead body also. You did not do it. God did it. But God did it through the discipline you offered.

I believe this is what Paul is talking about when he says, "Work out your own salvation with fear and trembling, for God is at work in you both to will and to work for God's good pleasure" (Phil 2:12-

13). You see, God has created us for a symbiotic relationship in our pilgrimage toward wholeness, and we have a responsibility in that relationship. But we must never deceive ourselves that our role alone is what brings about the transformation. Paul says we are to work out our salvation *with fear and trembling* because it is in our nature to take credit for the results. It is in our nature to take over the project and to turn it into a self-help project, a do-it-yourself operation. This temptation to works righteousness lurks at the heart of all our genuine spiritual disciplines. Paul, being the Pharisee that he was, knew the danger of that route.

And so those individualized spiritual disciplines to which the Spirit of God calls us in the midst of our deadness are our offerings of loving response and obedience through which God works by grace to transform our deadness into wholeness in the image of Christ. Our dead body is made alive through the Spirit who dwells within us.

I hope you can see now something of the way in which these individual, private disciplines are supported, nurtured and encouraged by the classical disciplines of the body of Christ. Our prayer, our spiritual reading, our worship, our daily office, our study, our fasting, our retreats are the structures that keep us open to the work of the Spirit of God in our lives and support and encourage the difficult work of our individual spiritual disciplines. And through all these means God lovingly holds us in the process of being conformed to the image of Christ for others, moves us from brokenness into wholeness.

Chapter 11

The Inner Dynamics of the Spiritual Disciplines

Gracious and loving God, I stand in awe of your infinite patience.
You desire my perfect wholeness. You are deeply desirous
to make me perfectly whole, even to the extent of entering into my
brokenness and taking its death into your own being
on the cross. And yet you never violate my independence, you never
trample upon my free will, you never usurp the integrity
of my being. You wait in infinite patience for me to open my life
to your cleansing, healing, liberating, transforming grace. You
wait for me to willingly cooperate with your purposes
for my wholeness. Help me, O my God, to offer to you the deep
inner yieldedness of my being that will enable my spiritual
disciplines to become avenues of your grace in me.

We have been noting, in our discussion of both the classical and the personal disciplines, that the greatest single danger in the spiritual disciplines is the temptation to turn them into works righteousness. Since the disciplines are activities we perform, from the very first performance there is the possibility that we will begin to think our performance will make the difference in our growth toward wholeness in Christ for others. There is a tremendous tension here. Without our performance of the disciplines, God is, for all practical purposes, left without any means of grace through which to effect transformation in our lives. But without God's transforming grace, our disciplines are empty, hollow motions, the form of godliness without the power. What is the solution?

The solution is found in the inner dynamics of how we engage in the disciplines, the deep inner posture of being we bring to the disciplines. This inner posture is expressed in the classical Christian spiritual tradition by the terms *silence, solitude* and *prayer.* As we will see, however, these terms carry far deeper significance than we usually attach to them. Usually these terms are associated with specific practices of spirituality, specific spiritual disciplines. Silence is fasting from speaking to listen to God; solitude is fasting from fellowship with others to be alone with God; prayer is a means of dialogue with God. However, when used to describe the inner posture of being we bring to spiritual disciplines, silence, solitude and prayer take on powerfully new and disturbing dimensions that probe the heart of our being and behavior.

Silence

We tend to think of *silence* as simply being still. But the silence of which the mothers and fathers of the church speak goes far beyond mere quietness. Their silence is the deep inner reversal of that grasping, controlling mode of being that so characterizes life in our culture. We have noted the powerful tendency in our culture to objectify everything and everyone around us—to make them objects that are to be arranged within our ordering of our world. We have also noted our penchant for then grasping those objects and bringing them under the agenda we have for the shaping of our world according to our own desires and purposes. Without the practice of silence, these cultural habits will attach themselves to our spiritual disciplines. The disciplines will become objects we employ in an attempt to produce our own transformation or in an attempt to manipulate God to bring about the changes we have decided are needed, or in an attempt to impress (and thereby control) others with our spirituality.

The practice of silence is the radical reversal of our cultural tendencies. Silence is bringing ourselves to a point of relinquishing to God our control of our relationship with God. Silence is a reversal of the whole possessing, controlling, grasping dynamic of trying to maintain control of our own existence. Silence is the inner act of letting it go.

A helpful means to this kind of silence is the prayer "Free me from care for myself." If used regularly as part of the daily office, God will gradually awaken us to the multiple layers of controlling, grasping "noise" in our lives: the defensive postures by which we justify our control of people and circumstances; the attack dynamics by which we extend and maintain our possession and control of others and our world; the indulgent habits by which we grasp things and others for ourselves; the manipulative practices by which we inflict our will on the world; and especially the ways in which we attempt to use God to support and justify these structures.

As the pervasiveness and subtlety of these structures of our being dawn upon us, the prayer "Free me from care for myself" will gradually become the cry of our heart to be free from these destructive bondages. The noise of self-rule will become intolerable, and we will begin to hunger for the silence of release to God. We will begin to yearn to be able to say with the psalmist,

O Lord, my heart is not proud
   nor haughty my eyes.
I have not gone after things too great
   nor marvels beyond me.

Truly I have set my soul
    in silence and peace. (Ps 131:1-2 Abbey Psalter)
We will be at the point of releasing control of our relationship with
God to God, where solitude begins.

Solitude

The second inner dynamic of our disciplines is *solitude.* We tend to
think of solitude as simply being alone. In the classical Christian
spiritual tradition, however, solitude is, in the silence of release,
beginning to face the deep inner dynamics of our being that make
us that grasping, controlling, manipulative person; beginning to
face our brokenness, our distortion, our darkness; and beginning to
offer ourselves to God at those points. Solitude is not simply draw-
ing away from others and being alone with God. This is part of
solitude. But more than this, it is being who we are with God and
acknowledging who we are to ourselves and to God.

The sterling biblical example of solitude is Jacob. Undoubtedly
you know the story of Jacob, whose name means "the supplanter,"
"the controller," "the manipulator." Jacob comes out of the womb
hanging onto to his brother's heel and continues climbing over people all along the way. Jacob manipulates his brother out of the
prized birthright that belonged to Esau as the firstborn. He manipulates his father to gain the blessing that traditionally went to the
firstborn. Even when Jacob encounters God at Bethel on his flight
from Esau's murderous rage, Jacob responds to God manipulatively:
"*If* God will be with me, and will keep me [safe] in this way that I
go, and will give me bread to eat and clothing to wear, so that I come
again to my father's house in peace, *then* the LORD shall be my God"
(Gen 28:20-21).

To be sure, Jacob often gets as good as he gives. His father-in-
law, Laban, is a pretty good manipulator himself, first manipulating
Jacob out of seven years of service and giving him Leah instead of
Rachel, then manipulating him out of seven more years for Rachel.

Jacob and Laban continue to go at each other, but finally Jacob's manipulation catches up with him. After he flees from Laban, having taken with him the best of the flocks, herds and cattle, his father-in-law catches up with him and they make an agreement. They set up a boundary stone and agree, in essence, "I'll stay on my side and you stay on your side. If you get caught on my side, you've had it. If I get caught on your side, I've had it" (see Gen 31:51-52).

The door is closed behind Jacob; he can't go back. He turns around and who is coming to meet him? Esau. Talk about being between a rock and a hard place; Esau isn't coming with flowers and garlands but with four hundred men. He is coming with an army. Where is Jacob going to go? There's nowhere to go. He can't turn back; Laban is behind him. He can't turn west; he's hemmed in by the Mediterranean. He can't turn east; he would die in the desert.

Notice what Jacob does at this point. He puts all that he has between himself and Esau: all of his cattle, all of his flocks, all of his herds, all of his servants, even his wives and children. Everything is expendable to save his own skin.

Jacob is left alone and, divested of everything, begins to experience the kind of silence and solitude we have been considering. He has nothing more with which to manipulate. He has lost it all now. It is all out there between him and his brother.

Jacob wrestles with God. Do you remember the outcome of that wrestling? God says to Jacob, "What is your name?" Now God knows Jacob's name. Since, biblically, name has to do with the nature of the one who is named, God is saying to Jacob, "What kind of person are you, really?"

And Jacob says, "I am the manipulator. I am Jacob, the supplanter."

At this moment Jacob's healing begins. The effect of his healing is seen immediately. In the next verse or two, we see Jacob out in front of everybody, going to meet Esau (Gen 33:3). Here is powerful evidence of the change that is taking place in Jacob. No longer is he manipulating others for his own benefit and safety. He is going out to take his medicine, whatever it is.

Jacob had to come to the point of solitude, the point of acknowledging before God the kind of person he was, before healing could
begin. And so do we! This is what solitude is: in the silence of
releasing control of our relationship with God to God, coming face
to face with the kind of person we are in the depths of our being;
seeing the depths of our grasping, manipulative, self-indulgent behavior; facing the brokenness, the darkness, the uncleanness that
is within; acknowledging our bondages, our false securities, our
posturing facades; and naming ourselves to God as this kind of
person.

Prayer

The final dynamic of spiritual disciplines is *prayer*. Prayer is the
outgrowth of both silence and solitude. In silence we let go of our
manipulative control. In solitude we face up to what we are in the
depths of our being. Prayer then becomes the offering of who we
are to God: the giving of that broken, unclean, grasping, manipulative self to God for the work of God's grace in our lives.

This is a yearning, hungering, wrestling prayer that enters into
the painful struggle between what we are and the crucifying desire
to become what God wants us to be. This kind of prayer struggles
with what we have been with others and hungers to be what God
intends us to be for them. This kind of prayer agonizes with what
we have allowed others to be in our lives and yearns to allow others
to be what God means for them to be for us.

Such silence, solitude and prayer form the deep inner rhythms of
the classical and personal spiritual disciplines on the journey from
awakening through purgation and illumination to union. And again
we come to realize that these dynamics cannot be maintained without the help, encouragement, support and accountability of our
sisters and brothers in Christ. Holistic growth into the image of
Christ for the sake of others is a corporate and social reality.

Part IV

Companions on the Way:

Corporate and Social Spirituality

In the previous sections of this book we have focused on the more personal aspects of spiritual formation. There is a danger that this could play into the privatizing and individualizing dynamics of our culture. Although from time to time I have highlighted the corporate nature of holistic spirituality, it's easy to lose sight of our full definition of spiritual formation as a process of being conformed to the image of Christ *for the sake of others*.

In this section we come back to the conclusion of our definition, focus on the *corporate* and *social* aspects of holistic spiritual formation and probe these two essential dimensions of spirituality. Our spiritual formation comes within a corporate and a social context. Our growth toward wholeness in Christ is for the sake of others within the body of Christ, that we might nurture one another into the wholeness of Christ. Our growth toward wholeness is also for the sake of others beyond the body of Christ, that the redeeming, healing, transforming love of God may be made known in a broken and hurting world.

The first chapter of this section (chapter twelve) will consider the corporate nature of being conformed to the image of Christ for the sake of others. Holistic spirituality enables us more and more to be agents of God's grace for our sisters and brothers in the body of Christ and, at the same time, increasingly allows them to be agents of God's grace for our growth toward wholeness.

The second chapter (thirteen) will probe the dynamics of social holiness, the role spiritual formation plays as we live in the midst of the social, political, economic, cultural dynamics of our society. John Wesley repeatedly affirmed that there can be no personal holiness without social holiness. The converse is also true: there can be no social holiness without personal holiness. If spiritual formation is, indeed, being conformed to the image of Christ for the sake of others, *the ultimate test of our spirituality lies in the nature of our life in the world with others.*

Chapter 12

Corporate Spirituality

*Gracious and loving God, we thank and praise you for what we
have been sharing together. We thank you for your
presence with us. For the work you have been doing in our
minds and hearts, for the ways you have been touching our lives,
known and unknown, we give you praise and thanks. And as we
come to the final aspects of our sharing, may we again,
by your grace, open our lives to you fully, completely, and give you
permission to do whatever you want to do in us through these
pages. Help us, in the depths of our hearts, to say yes to you in a
fuller, more complete way. Guide us by the anointing of your
Spirit, that we may receive what you have for us.*

---

*C*orporate spirituality is a name for our spiritual pilgrimage together
in the church, the body of Christ. In the second section of this book
we considered the interplay of our personality preferences. We saw
that even the particular creation gifts God has given to each one of
us have corporate dimensions. Remember the paraphrase of 1 Corinthians 12:14-26:

For the body of Christ does not consist of one temperament, but
of many. If the INTJ should say, "Because I am not an ESFP, I
do not belong to the body," that would not make it any less a part

of the body. And if the ISTP should say, "Because I'm not an ESTJ, I do not belong to the body," that would not make it any less a part of the body. If the whole body were an INFP, where would be the ENTJ? If the whole body were an INTP, where would be the ENFJ? But as it is, God arranged the temperaments in the body of Christ—each one of them as God chose. If all were a single temperament, where would the body be? As it is, there are many temperaments, yet one body. The INFJ cannot say to the ESTP, "I have no need of you." Nor again the ESFJ to the ISFP, "I have no need of you." God has so adjusted the body that there may be no discord within it, but that the temperaments may have the same care for one another. If one temperament suffers, all suffer together. If one temperament is honored, all rejoice together. Now you are the body of Christ and individual temperaments of it.

While this may be slightly tongue-in-cheek, I believe it keeps faith with the essence of Paul's point. Our unique individuality is one of the gifts we bring to the body of Christ. Others need the gift of our preference type in their growth toward wholeness. We need the gifts of others' preference types in our growth toward wholeness. The diversity in our temperament types is part of the glorious diversity of the body of Christ, in which God nurtures us to wholeness.

Yet how difficult it is for us to rejoice in this diversity— how easy to try to squeeze one another into molds of our own making instead of allowing each to contribute his or her uniqueness to the body and to our own growth toward wholeness in Christ.

In the community of faith, those who prefer introversion ought to provide a nurturing balance of reflection for the extraverts, who prefer action. The extraverts, in turn, help to meet the introverts' need for action and involvement, for the nurturing of that less preferred side of their temperament. Here, too, those who prefer sensing ought to provide "reality therapy" for the intuitives, who tend to overlook the details of sensory data. Meanwhile, the introverts supply the gift of intuition and vision that keeps the sensing persons from getting bogged down by the "facts." Again, in corporate spirituality those who prefer the thinking approach ought to provide the gift of logic, reason and objectivity for those whose preference for a feeling approach may result in sentimental or emotional responses to issues. But the feeling persons' compassion provides a nurturing gift for thinking persons, who tend to be cold and impersonal. Finally, in the community of faith the "perceiving" persons ought to provide the gift of spontaneity and openness for the "judging" persons, who tend to get stuck in ruts of habit and order. "Judging" persons, in turn, provide the gift of discipline and structure for the "perceiving" persons, who tend to go with the flow and live for the moment.

Returning to Paul's metaphor, we are individual cells of the body of Christ. Our wholeness depends on the creative and nurturing interplay of our individual gifts. It is said that one cold and gloomy day, Dwight L. Moody visited a man who had expressed some interest at one of Moody's meetings. Moody was ushered into a comfortable room with a fire blazing on the hearth. After some gracious preliminary conversation, the man began to argue that it was possible for a person to be a Christian without participating in the life of the church. As he made his elaborate and detailed arguments, Moody leaned forward in his chair, took the poker and pulled a flaming coal from the fire out onto the stone hearth. Moody watched as the coal slowly dimmed and went out. He then turned and looked at the man, without saying anything. After a long pause, the man said, "Mr. Moody, you have made your point!"

We can no more be conformed to the image of Christ outside of corporate spirituality than a coal can continue to burn bright outside of the fire.

Building One Another Up
In the third section of this book we considered the dynamics of

spiritual disciplines and saw how essential the corporate dimension is in maintaining any kind of faithfulness in our spiritual disciplines. In the first place, the community of faith is the living reality within which the classical spiritual disciplines nurture us and provide the support structure for our personal disciplines. When we don't feel like worshiping, the community should carry us along in its worship. When we can't seem to pray, community prayer should enfold us. When the Scripture seems closed for us, the community should keep on reading, affirming and incarnating it around us.

In the second place, when God begins to work with us at the deep levels of our incompleteness and brokenness, our bondage and sin, we need the body of Christ to support, encourage, challenge and nurture us toward wholeness. We may be able to work through some of our bondage and brokenness alone with God. But when God begins to deal with some of the deep distortions of our being, we need others. In such times we confess our sin to one another, bear one another's burdens and become for one another means of grace to maintain the discipline through which God can bring us to wholeness. Such transformation is hard for us. The idea of corporate spirituality moves powerfully against the grain of our deeply encultured individualized, privatized understanding of spirituality.

Kenneth Leech touches upon this pointedly:

We have seen a massive revival of false spiritualities. Since the 1960s an epidemic of 'private religion' has gripped parts of North America and Europe. The private religions offer a range of techniques and methodologies by which salvation and enlightenment can be acquired. Many of these religions have become wealthy and flourishing corporations. The sale of enlightenment has become highly profitable. Indeed, businessmen in the United States have supported some meditation schools on the grounds that they contribute to profits by increasing wakefulness, efficiency, and compliance in the workforce.[1]

Now consider these words from Leech:

Such private religions are invariably non-prophetic. They do not disturb the economic and political order and so they fit easily and comfortably into the culture of capitalism. The god they offer is a *private god*, a *wholly inward god*. In the context of public enterprise and private religion, spirituality can quickly degenerate into a search for better, perhaps more thrilling and unusual, experiences. So much of the current interest in "the God within" has moved in the direction of a narrow and limited understanding of God and of the nature of religion.[2]

I think you can see and sense here the kind of individualizing and privatizing danger that faces us, and the corresponding difficulty with understanding the corporate and social dimensions of spirituality.

Paying the Price

Corporate spirituality is costly. It is much easier to let everybody "do their own thing." At least it seems much easier. I hope you were able to see from our discussion of spiritual disciplines that, left to ourselves, we do not have the resources to maintain the disciplines that God uses as means of grace to transform us to wholeness in the image of Christ. And yet it seems easier to break into like-minded factions than to allow God to use us as agents of grace for one another. Allowing God to use us in this way is costly, for it involves an investment of ourselves for others, a disclosure of ourselves to others. When we begin to understand what confessing our sins to one another means (Jas 5:16), we begin to realize the level of vulnerability and disclosure that is involved in genuine corporate spirituality.

Most of us already practice some corporate spirituality, but it tends to be very superficial and external. We never move with one another into the depths of our being, where God can do the crucifying work of nurturing us into wholeness.

Maintaining the Mystery

Here is another insight from Leech. "Whatever we may think of it, 'the modern world is above all else a religious world . . . not really secularized at all. . . . This is essentially a world of the sacred.' What is different is that the sacred is now the private. . . . it is this combination of private religion and effective nihilism which most marks our age."[3] What Leech means by "effective nihilism" is that in the privatization of religion, one becomes a world unto oneself— a privateness that, in effect, annihilates the rest of the world. We become so ingrown upon ourselves that we miss the reality of the world "out there."

Leech then raises a crucial dimension of holistic spirituality:

The essential difference between orthodox Christianity and the various heretical systems is that orthodoxy is rooted in paradox. Heretics, as Irenaeus saw, reject paradox in favor of a false clarity and precision. But true faith can only grow and mature if it includes the elements of paradox and creative doubt. Hence the insistence of orthodoxy that God cannot be known by the mind, but is known in the obscurity of faith, in the way of ignorance, in the darkness. Such doubt is not the enemy of faith but an essential element within it. For faith in God does not bring the false peace of answered questions and resolved paradoxes. Rather, it can be seen as a process of "unceasing interrogation." . . . The spirit enters into our lives and puts disturbing questions. Without such creative doubt, religion becomes hard and cruel, degenerating into the spurious security which breeds intolerance and persecution. Without doubt, there is loss of inner reality and of inspirational power to religious language. The whole of spiritual life must suffer from, and be seriously harmed by, the repression of doubt.[4]

Leech reveals here another aspect of privatized and superficial spirituality. Where one has all the right answers, all the easy answers, all the quick fixes, there is no room for mystery. There is no room for paradox. And if there is no room for mystery there is no room for God, because God is the ultimate mystery.

One part of genuine spiritual pilgrimage is coming to the point where we let go of our limited concept of God. We let go of that box within which we have enclosed God, and we open ourselves to allow God to be whatever God wants to be in our life. When we do this, we also lose our former awareness and sense of God's presence. We lose our grasp upon God.

Here, you see, is where faith enters into mystery, into the dark night of the soul. And here we need one another, in the strength of corporate spirituality, to encourage, to sustain, to support, to enable us to let go of our control of God, to let God be God, and to dwell in the mystery.

Without a holistic corporate spirituality, there is a powerful tendency to become heterodox or heretical. Corporate spirituality is essential, because privatization always fashions a spirituality that in some way allows us to maintain control of God. Without brothers and sisters to call us to accountability, we will work powerfully to maintain that control. Jesus' dialogue with Nicodemus (Jn 3:1-21) was such a call to accountability.

The Matter of Control

There is a tremendous lesson for us in Jesus' call to Nicodemus to be "born again." But to appreciate what is going on here, we have to start at John 2:23.

John 2 starts with the wedding in Cana, then records the cleansing of the temple in Jerusalem. John 3 tells the story of Nicodemus. But John 2:23-25 seems to stick out like a sore thumb. You wonder why on earth John inserts this little remark between the accounts of the cleansing of the temple and the encounter with Nicodemus. "While Jesus was among the Jerusalemites in the feast of Passover, many believed in his name as they beheld the signs which he did. But Jesus did not believe[5] himself to them for he knew all, and because he did not need for anyone to bear witness of man,[6] for he himself knew what was in man. Now there was a man of the Pharisees named Nicodemus . . ."

As I was wrestling with these three verses, it dawned upon me how they fit into the structure of John's Gospel at this point. The problem they introduce is that people believed in Jesus while Jesus did not "believe himself to them." This last phrase is especially puzzling. What does John mean when he says, "Jesus did not believe himself to them"?

The statement takes on crucial significance when you realize that "believing" is focal in the Gospel of John. About 40 percent of all the appearances of the verb *believe* in the New Testament are in the Gospel of John—99 of 240 New Testament appearances. You don't have to read very far into John to discover this. In 1:7, speaking of John the Baptist, the Evangelist says that the Baptist was sent "to bear witness to the light *that all might believe* through him." Then in 1:12, speaking of Jesus, John says, "As many as received him, *who believed in his name*, he gave power to become children of God." We all know why John wrote his Gospel; he tells us in 20:31: "These things are written in order *that you might believe* that Jesus is the Messiah, the Son of God, and *believing*, you might have life in his name."

If you go through the whole Gospel of John, in practically every paragraph you'll find something about believing. Believing is vital in John's presentation of Christ. So when you come to these verses where a group of people "believe" in Jesus, and John turns right around and says Jesus does not believe himself to them, you begin to realize that something of vital significance is being said. John is pointing to a failure of believing. The people "believed" in Jesus, but in a way that prevented Jesus from entering into vital relationship with them—"believing" himself to them. A closure of that belief relationship from Jesus' side was not possible.

What was the problem? *Nicodemus is the example of the problem!* This is why it is necessary to keep the noninclusive language in 2:23-25: "Jesus did not believe himself to them, for he knew all, and because he did not need for anyone to bear witness of *man*, for he himself knew what was in *man*. Now there was a *man* of the Pharisees named Nicodemus." Do you see John's flow—how he connects these accounts? Nicodemus is the example of what is wrong in those who believe in Jesus in a way that does not allow Jesus to enter into vital relationship with them—to "believe himself to them."

Now, the first thing we are told about Nicodemus is that he is a Pharisee. We know *what* he is before we know *who* he is. And this is significant, because the Pharisees were the holiness movement of Jesus' day. The Pharisees get terribly bad press in Christian circles. When we hear "Pharisee," immediately we know that is a negative term. But the Pharisees were people who had committed them-selves unreservedly to living in priestly holiness, to living in such absolute, total obedience to the Torah that they could say with Paul, "as to righteousness under the law, [we are] blameless" (Phil 3:6). And they were doing it! You might say they were the leaders of the spiritual formation movement in Jesus' day. And Nicodemus is not just any run-of-the-mill Pharisee. He is a ruler of the Jews (Jn 3:1), and Jesus calls him a teacher of Israel (Jn 3:10).

So what is Nicodemus's problem? And what is the problem of those for whom a closure of the belief relationship from Jesus' side was not possible? Well, Nicodemus obviously believed in God. Nic-odemus's whole life was devoted to God. Yet it is to this kind of person that Jesus says, "You must be born again" (Jn 3:6).

The church in North America has taken this passage completely out of context. We tend to think of it in terms of the non-Christian, the "unsaved," and give it an evangelistic twist. Now there is noth-ing wrong in using this phrase evangelistically, but when we look at it in its context, it has a much more profound impact upon those of us who are seeking to be pilgrims of the faith. Because that's

what Nicodemus was. Nicodemus probably would put most of us
to shame in the quality of his spiritual life.

Jesus says to Nicodemus, "You must be born again." Then Jesus
starts talking with him about the life of one born of the Spirit and
illustrates it with the wind.[7] "The wind blows where it wills, and
you hear the sound of it, but you don't know where it comes from
or where it goes" (Jn 3:8). This is the vital clue to Nicodemus's
problem.

Nicodemus had his relationship with God all wrapped up under his own control.
Instead of being led by the presence of God (Spirit) in his life,
Nicodemus himself determined the nature of his relationship with
God. While relationship with God was the primary focus of Nicode-
mus's life, Nicodemus controlled the nature of the relationship.

Paul describes this aspect of his own life as a Pharisee in Philippians 3. If John had not told us that this person in chapter 3 of his
Gospel was Nicodemus, we might well have suspected it to be Paul,
because Paul's litany in Philippians epitomizes the perspective of a
Pharisee like Nicodemus: "Circumcised on the eighth day [in precise
obedience to the Torah], of the race of Israel [not a Gentile], of the
tribe of Benjamin [no mixed blood], a Hebrew born of Hebrews
[descent from Abraham], according to the Torah a Pharisee [the
strictest of observant Jews], according to zeal a persecutor of the
church [to purify Israel from this 'heresy'], as to righteousness [right
relationship with God] under the Torah, blameless" (Phil 3:5-6).

Then listen to what Paul goes on to say: "Whatever benefit I had
from this [in my relationship with God] I considered as loss. . . .
Indeed, I considered all to be loss on account of the surpassing
worth of knowing Christ Jesus as my Lord [a new relationship with
God] . . so that I might be found in him not having my right
relationship with God ["righteousness"] which [results] from [obe-
dience to] the Torah, but that [right relationship with God] which
comes through the faith of Christ" (Phil 3:7-9). Here we see that
Paul had come to recognize the radical reorientation that had taken

place when he entered into that belief relationship with Jesus as Messiah. Paul had given up a relationship with God based on his own control and had given control to God. Prior to this, Paul had pursued a right relationship with God (righteousness) of his own, based upon his faithful observance of the Torah—an observance of such absolute obedience in Paul's eyes that he could say, "I was blameless." In Paul's perspective, God could hold nothing against him. But Paul came to realize that he was in control of that relationship.

Like Paul, Nicodemus was in control of his relationship with God. So Jesus is saying, "Nicodemus, you must let God have control of the relationship. You must let the wind of the Spirit blow your life along God's path, not yours."

This was the problem with those people John called attention to at the end of chapter 2. They "believed" in Jesus, but not in a way that allowed Jesus to "believe" himself to them. There was no closure in the relationship. This may be what John intimates by noting that their "belief" was based on the signs Jesus did. They may have wanted Jesus to do signs for them—to bring God's power into *their* agendas, to get God to fulfill *their* purposes.

Matthew gives us another glimpse of the same reality. At the close of the Sermon on the Mount, Jesus speaks of a group of people who will appear before him on the day of judgment. They will say, "Lord, Lord, did we not prophesy in your name, and cast out demons in your name, and do many mighty works in your name?" (Mt 7:22). And Jesus does not contradict them. He does not say, "No! You did not!" Instead, Jesus says to them, "Depart from me, you evildoers, *I never knew you*" (Mt 7:23). These are obviously people who believed in Jesus, and their lives had been shaped by that "belief." They had spent their lives doing things "in Jesus' name." Their lives, apparently, had been marked by rigorous religiosity and filled with religious activities. But Jesus reveals that their activities did not spring from a vital relationship with him. They were in control of the relationship they had with Jesus. These "believers" were operating out of their own agendas, not in response to a relationship in which Jesus was truly Lord.

Jesus picks this up later in John's Gospel, when he says to his disciples, "You did not choose me. I chose you" (15:16). There is a radical difference between the two halves of this statement. If we have chosen Jesus, we retain control of the relationship. We determine what role Jesus has in our life. We determine what role Jesus plays in our vocation, in our relationships, in our leisure time, in our recreational activities, in our selection of reading materials, in our choice of movies and TV programs, in our friendships. But if we allow Jesus to choose us, there is inherent in that action a relinquishment of control of the relationship to Jesus. That is what Jesus was doing with Nicodemus; calling Nicodemus out of his privatized religion into a release of the control of his relationship with God to God.

Control and Relationship with Others

The relinquishment of the control of our relationship with God to God is the essence, I think, of moving out of our privatized, individualized spirituality and into corporate spirituality. When we do release control of our relationship with God to God, we discover that God responds! Soon we come into contact with others who become agents of grace in our growth toward wholeness in Christ, while we become agents of God's grace in *their* growth. We are set in a whole new frame of reference with respect to others.

When we are in control of our relationship with God, when we try to maintain a privatized spirituality, we have to maintain a defensive posture toward others. We have to protect ourselves against them because we sense, unconsciously if not consciously, that there is a fatal flaw somewhere in our privatized spirituality—and anyone might disclose it. I have to keep you at arm's length lest you reveal the weakness, the flaw, in my privatized spirituality.

But if such disclosure is no longer my concern, if I can release that obsessive self-control of my relationship with God to God, then I no longer have to fear you. I can welcome your insights into my incompleteness, because you can be a means of God's grace to awaken me to the blind spots in my life and my relationship with God. I can receive the gifts of your temperament preference and openly share mine with you. I can disclose to you the growing edges of my spiritual pilgrimage, the tender places of my brokenness and the hard places of my bondage, and receive God's healing, liberating grace through you. You can become a means of transforming grace, and I can welcome you. I do not have to protect myself against you. I can also commit myself to you in your brokenness and bondage and allow God to work through me in God's way, not my manipulative one.

Several years ago, a fellow member of a spiritual formation group—I'll call him Peter—came to me with a problem Peter was facing three very significant opportunities for ministry. One of them had already been a source of fruitful and enriching ministry for two years before Peter entered seminary. The other two were radically different—unknown territory. Peter was having great difficulty in discerning God's will for the future. Which opportunity should be taken?

As I probed gently, I began to realize that Peter really wanted to return to the ministry that had been so fruitful in the past. When I asked, "What you want to do is return to your former ministry, isn't it?" he said, "Yes, more than anything else in the world." I realized that Peter's "possession" of that ministry was preventing openness to God's guidance.

Because of the level of trust and caring that had developed in our spiritual formation group over the years, I was able to say, "You will never have clarity on God's will for you here until you are willing to surrender that old ministry to God. Even if it is God's will for you now, you cannot go there in God's will until you first surrender your desire for it."

Tears poured from Peter's eyes as he acknowledged, "Yes—I know." It took a month of struggle and wrestling, but one day he came to me and said, "I've surrendered the old ministry to God. I'm ready to do whatever God wants me to do."

Because Peter didn't have to be defensive or protective of self with me, he was free to hear a hard word that opened him to becoming available to God.

Perhaps one of the questions we need to ask ourselves as we wrestle with the corporate nature of holistic spirituality is whether we're ready to relinquish control of our relationship with God to God. Are we really willing to let God be God in our life? I don't know what that means for you. You have to wrestle this through yourself, preferably with a group of brothers and sisters who will help you be honest. In my spiritual formation group we wrestle with this constantly. We see in one another, and we help one another see in ourselves, the subtle ways we avoid the question and maintain control of that relationship instead of letting God be God.

Life in the Body of Christ

Corporate spirituality is life in the body of Christ, not as a metaphor but the living reality of the presence of Christ in the community of faith. As individual "cells" of the body of Christ, we each have unique gifts of temperament preference, personality and character that exist for the welfare of the entire body. We are to be means of God's grace to the other cells in the body and, in turn, receive from our companion cells what God graces to us through them. The areas of damage within us, our bondages, are to be healed, liberated and transformed through the support and nurture of the other cells of the body. Our personal spiritual disciplines, rather than separating us from the other cells in the body, become a means of binding us together in love and support as we seek each other's growth into wholeness. Meanwhile, the corporate disciplines of the body supply the supporting nurture of Life for each of the individual cells.

It is only in the body of Christ that we are constantly challenged to allow God to be in control of the relationship we have with God. In fact, only as living cells in the body of Christ can we truly allow God to be in control. As soon as we take control of our relationship with God, we begin to isolate ourselves from the other cells and become a cancerous, destructive presence in the body.

I hope you can see from what we have considered in this chapter that corporate spirituality is the only context within which we can grow toward wholeness in the image of Christ.

Chapter 13

Social Spirituality

*O God of peoples, nations and history; you who became incarnate
in the midst of economic, social and political injustice; you who call
us to incarnate the reality of your kingdom in the midst of the
world's destructive values, structures and dynamics: we confess that
we would much rather limit our relationship with you to the comfortable confines of our own insulated world. We are prone to
withdraw and to create islands of security within which we can
live in some degree of peace and comfort without having to see the
pain and anguish of the world outside. We are tempted to limit our
spirituality to the narrow boundaries of our self-circumscribed
world. O God of justice and mercy, help us see that to be
conformed to the image of Christ is to be thrust out into the world
as agents of your redeeming, healing, liberating, transforming
grace. Help us to see that our growth toward wholeness in Christ
cannot move toward its fruition apart from our life in the world.
Guide us in our consideration of this reality in this chapter, and
help us to be open and responsive to what you are saying to us.*

---

*T*o be conformed to the image of Christ for others not only calls
us to the fullness of life in the body of Christ, as we saw in the
previous chapter; it also thrusts us into the world as agents of God's
healing, transforming grace. *Social spirituality* designates our spiritual

pilgrimage within and for the culture we live in. John Wesley repeatedly stressed that there is no personal holiness without social holiness.

We must be very careful not to make this a one-way equation—it works both ways. Just as there is no personal holiness without social holiness, so also there is no social holiness without personal holiness. The mistake we have made is to break the two apart. Some people emphasize personal holiness, others emphasize social holiness. The problem is that neither group ends up with *any* holiness.

When persons move exclusively toward personal holiness, the result is a very peculiar kind of piety, to put it gently. Their lives tend to become compartmentalized. Their "spiritual life" is in one compartment, their daily life in the world in another. There is an infinite variety of spiritually unhealthy patterns that emerge from this. At one extreme are judgmental, self-righteous persons who looks down their pious noses at the world in its brokenness and bondage. At the other extreme is the pious libertine—profoundly spiritual in the spiritual compartment and just as worldly in the social compartment.

Kenneth Leech again pointedly diagnoses our condition, picking up some of the same dynamics we looked at in corporate spirituality and applying them to social spirituality. He says, "In our day Christianity is widely seen as a religion of personal pronouns, a purely individual faith; and this understanding is felt to be traditional, though it is in fact of recent origin. The traditional social doctrine of orthodox Christianity has been largely forgotten and replaced by an individualistic theology."[1] Privatization of faith is as damaging in the social arena as it is in the community of faith—individualized spirituality undercuts any vital witness in the social order we live in.

When persons move exclusively toward social holiness, the result can become a very manipulative, destructive kind of works righteousness. I will never forget a young man who participated in a two-year spiritual formation process with which I was involved. We sat together one day and shared our spiritual journeys. He was a young African-American who had been engaged in a very creative and effective social ministry in a major metropolitan area. I asked him, "Why did you decide to participate in this event?"

He replied, "Because after all of the years I spent on the leading edge of social justice, I began to realize that I was absolutely empty within. Even though I believed in what I was doing and believed that God was in what I was doing, I had lost all sense of God's presence. My life was empty. I was burned out. I began reading some of the great social reformers of the Christian tradition. I discovered the key to their success was that they had a deep personal relationship with God. They had a personal piety that fueled their social piety." Then he added, "I didn't have that, and I realized that I needed it."

A Biblical Tension

The Old Testament prophets continually remind God's people that the worship of God is incompatible with social, economic or political injustice. Worship of God is to result in a focal concern for the welfare of one's neighbors and community. Attempting to worship God while closing one's eyes to dehumanizing injustices in the social, political and economic realms—or, worse, while engaging in practices that contribute to injustice—is regularly denounced as totally unacceptable. Iniquity joined with solemn assembly is an abomination to God.

The New Testament regularly conjoins love for God with love for one's neighbor, and indicates that the godliness that is pure and faultless is to look after marginalized and powerless people (Jas 1:27). As Leech puts it, "To dissociate the divine justice from the struggle for justice within the human community is to make nonsense of the biblical record."[2]

Biblical spirituality calls us away from the individualized, privatized forms of the raith that enable us to isolate ourselves from the brokenness and bondage of the world around us. Biblical spirituality calls us into a relationship with God that thrusts us out into the world as agents of healing, liberating grace. Of course, the first thing biblical spirituality does is to unmask the façades of piety behind which we hid our own brokenness and bondage. Biblical spirituality probes our complicity in the injustice of the world, our own contribution to the dehumanizing perspectives and practices that shape our portion of the world. This is why it is so much easier to take refuge in privatized forms of spirituality.

A genuinely Christian spirituality is not only rooted in a vital, growing relationship with God at the heart of one's being but also incarnated in the reality of the social, economic and political context in which one lives. Such spirituality is relevant, revolutionary, transforming.

But while our spirituality must be lived out in the world, it must avoid becoming the captive of its context. Whenever our spirituality becomes captive to the world in which we live, it becomes a proponent and defender of the status quo. Leech states it forcefully: "But, what happens when theology becomes captured by its context, by the prevailing culture? Theology, and the institutional church in which theological reflection takes place, then becomes a resource of the culture and no longer its critic. Theology becomes the servant of the social order, the God of justice is tamed and put at the service of organized injustice."[3]

There must be a creative tension between our spiritual pilgrimage and the world in which it is lived out. If we attempt to undo this difficult tension, we move either into an "unworldly" spirituality that isolates us from the world or into a "worldly" spirituality that insulates us from the radical demands of a vital relationship with God. In the first resolution God becomes our private possession, in the second a domesticated support for the status quo. In neither instance is God allowed to be the One who calls us out of life in the world on its terms in order to thrust us back into the world on God's terms.

Holistic spirituality is a situation of being never at home yet fully at home in the social order. We are never at home, for our lives are not shaped by the values, structures and dynamics of the world around us; yet we are fully at home, for in the midst of those destructive and dehumanizing values of the world we live out the values, structures and dynamics of God's new order of being in Christ. "Following the leadership of Jesus, his Church needs to stand as a sign of contradiction and of conflict, affecting and, as it were, upsetting through the power of the Gospel, mankind's criteria of judgment, determining values, points of interest, lines of thought, sources of inspiration, and models of life which are in contrast with the Word of God and the plan of salvation."[4]

Holy Living in an Unholy World

In Scripture we see this reality powerfully manifested in John's vision set forth in the book of Revelation. John's vision is not about the rapture, and it is not a blueprint of the future. Instead, it is a profound vision of what it means to be a citizen of New Jerusalem in the midst of a world that is shaped by the destructive values and dehumanizing powers of Fallen Babylon. This is what social spirituality is all about.

But it is impossible for us, as citizens of New Jerusalem, to be the agents of God's healing, transforming and yes, *disturbing* presence in the life of the world unless we are also bound together in a way that gives us clarity of discernment. We see some of the danger this role poses for us in the letters to the seven churches in Revelation. I call them the good, the bad and the ugly.[5]

There are two good churches. They are living lives of faithful New Jerusalem citizenship in the midst of Fallen Babylon. Jesus has nothing to say against them. But it is interesting how they are described. (If you are a proponent of the "prosperity gospel," cover your eyes, because you will not like what God's Word has to say here.)

The first good church is the one in Smyrna (Rev 2:8-11). To this faithful church Jesus says, "I know your tribulation and your poverty . . . and the slander of those who say they are Jews and are not, but are synagogues of Satan. Do not fear what you are about to suffer. The devil is about to throw some of you into prison, that you may be tested, and for ten days you will have tribulation. Be faithful unto death." I don't know about you, but there are a lot of words here that do not make me very comfortable—*tribulation, poverty, slander, fear, suffer, prison, tested, death*. And this is a *faithful* church!

Do you want to read about the church that is rich and prosperous and needs nothing? That is one of the bad churches—Laodicea (Rev 3:14-22). To this prosperous church Jesus says, "You do not know that you are wretched, pitiable, poor, blind and naked." There is a radical reversal of values here.

To the other good church, Philadelphia, Jesus says, "I know you have but little power. . . . You have not denied my name [in the face of persecution]. . . . You have kept my word of patient endurance" (Rev 3:8-10). Again we see a church that is experiencing tribulation at the hands of Fallen Babylon. To the other bad church, Sardis, Jesus says, "I know your works, that you have the reputation of being alive; you are dead" (Rev 3:1). These folks have no problems with their life in the world; they have the name of being alive, they are an active church. But not really, you see. Again, there is a radical reversal of values.

Then there are three ugly churches. These churches are an interesting mixture of faithful discipleship as citizens of New Jerusalem and destructive accommodation to the values and dynamics of Fallen Babylon. For instance, to Pergamum Jesus says, "I know where you dwell, where Satan's throne is [the center of emperor worship in Asia Minor was located in Pergamum at this time], and you have held my name and not denied my faith in the days of Antipas, my faithful martyr who was slain in your midst" (Rev 2:13). It sounds as if they have a sound spiritual pilgrimage as a church, as if they are faithful citizens of New Jerusalem in the midst of Pergamum, "where Satan dwells." But then Jesus takes them to task for tolerating idolatry and fornication in their fellowship. They are accommodating themselves to the values and lifestyle of Fallen Babylon.

In his vision, John sees that there are two orders of being that shape human existence. One is called New Jerusalem, the other is called Fallen Babylon. New Jerusalem is the place where people are nurtured into wholeness in the image of Christ and find fulfillment at the deepest levels of their being. Fallen Babylon is the order of being that is inherently destructive of human wholeness. In his own day John sees these two orders of being manifested: New Jerusalem in the life of the church, and Fallen Babylon in the values and lifestyle of the Roman Empire. But we also see in John's vision that the Harlot, who for him was Rome, is also the mother of harlots (17:15)—there are more "harlots" coming after Rome.

There is in every age of history a new generation of the Harlot, whose destructive values and dehumanizing social structures form the Fallen Babylon in which each generation of the church is called to live as faithful citizens of God's New Jerusalem. John sees this as the context of our social spirituality. As you work through John's vision, you discover that the church becomes the active presence of God in the midst of the fallen order. Through the church God is a confronting and challenging presence, disturbing and disruptive as well as redemptive and healing. This is what Leech points to when he says, "Christian realism . . . is motivated not by a theology which seeks to baptize a current social order but by a theology of dissatisfaction with *all* current social orders, a theology of the God-inspired future which draws future vision into present reality."[6] As our lives are increasingly shaped toward wholeness in the image of Christ by the values, dynamics and structures of God's order, we come into conflict with the dehumanizing and manipulative structures and dynamics of the fallen order within which we live. We begin to live holy lives in an unholy world.

John envisions this powerfully in his vision of the New Jerusalem coming down out of heaven from God (Rev 21:9—22:5). John sees a huge, cubic city (the twelve thousand stadia are about fourteen hundred miles), and it is the dwelling place of God. Now why is this city, the dwelling place of God, cubic? It is the Holy of Holies. In the Jerusalem temple, the Holy of Holies was a cubic space (see 1 Kings 6:20) where God's presence dwelt. John is seeing that the new covenant community is the new Holy of Holies. Paul uses the same image when he speaks of the church not only as a holy temple but as the dwelling place of God in the Spirit (Eph 2:21-22).

Now, if you take a map of the Mediterranean, cut out a square fourteen hundred miles on a side to the scale of the map and lay the square over the map with its center on the Island of Patmos, where John received his vision, you discover that the western edge falls right about where Rome is, the eastern edge falls along the eastern boundary of the Roman Empire near Jerusalem, and the northern and southern edges follow the northern and southern boundaries of the eastern Roman Empire. The real significance of this, however, is that at the time John received the vision, every living Christian lived within that square! The church had not yet moved beyond those boundaries. John was seeing that the church in his day was the citizenship of New Jerusalem in the midst of the Fallen Babylon of the Roman Empire.

John's vision has to do with the dynamics of these two orders, how they contend against one another and, particularly, what it means to be a faithful citizen of New Jerusalem in the midst of Fallen Babylon. Such a life—lived by the values and perspectives of God's new order of being in Christ in the midst of the destructive values of Fallen Babylon—is the essence of all social spirituality.

Life in New Jerusalem
Social spirituality is rooted in the integrity of our life together as

citizens of New Jerusalem. If we don't have a corporate spirituality of accountability to one another for our pilgrimage toward wholeness in the image of Christ, we are going to be subverted by the values and the perspectives of the fallen order around us. As a church we will fall captive to the culture.

Now, this does not mean that the church sets itself against the culture. The church is not called primarily to be confrontive, but to be obedient and faithful to God's presence and purposes in the culture. The result will be confrontive, but that should not be the purpose. Our purpose should be to live out the values and dynamics of New Jerusalem in the midst of the values and dynamics of Fallen Babylon. When we do this, Fallen Babylon is going to be disturbed. Fallen Babylon will not appreciate the bringing to light of its value system. Yet the confrontation comes not because we seek it, but because falsehood cannot stand in the presence of truth.

This is why there can be no true social holiness without personal holiness. Personal holiness comes as a result of the spiritual journey we have described in the rest of this book. The deep commitment of our beings to God, the growing life of responsive relationship with God, the increasing work of God's transforming grace in our brokenness and bondage all lead us toward the wholeness of conformity to Christ. Such personal holiness, however, is conformity to One whose life was given unconditionally for others. Such personal holiness is nurtured in a corporate community of faith. Without the nurturing growth and accountability of the community of faith, we will never have the clarity of discernment that will enable us to walk in Christ's way in the midst of a world that would try to bend us out of that way. Corporate spirituality is the only hope for genuine social spirituality.

Conversely, corporate spirituality will wither on the vine if it does not reach out into the world. A corporate spirituality that insulates and protects us from the world is close to death. Jesus describes such a corporate spirituality in his word to the church in

Ephesus (Rev 2:1-7). Here is a church that receives tremendous commendation: "I know your works, your toil and your endurance. You cannot tolerate evil. You have tested those who claim to be apostles and are not, and have found them to be false. You have endured, you have borne up for my name's sake, you have not grown weary." This sounds like a community of faith that has it all together. They are "keeping the faith" and being careful not to be tainted by the world around them. But then Jesus says to them, "I have this against you, that you have forsaken the love you had at first. Remember from what you have fallen. Repent and do the works you did at first. If you do not repent, I will come and remove your lampstand from its place." In spite of its good report, this community of faith is about to be snuffed out.

Acts portrays the Ephesian church as having such powerful outreach into their world that they were seriously disrupting the economic order. So many people were coming to faith in Christ that the metalsmiths, whose livelihood depended upon sales of figurines as votive offerings to the temple of Diana, were going out of business. They stirred up the city of Ephesus with concern for this radical upheaval of the status quo. Not only was the city of Ephesus affected, but, as Luke tells us, the whole province of Asia was reached by the Word of the Lord (Acts 19:10).

So what was the problem in Ephesus? It was the lack of the love the Ephesian Christians had had at first. Somewhere between the vital, transforming social witness described in Acts and Jesus' word to the church in John's vision, the Ephesian church had become a community of cold orthodoxy—maintaining its "faithfulness" in isolation from the world, not allowing the world to subvert it, but having no transforming impact upon the world around. Corporate spirituality without social spirituality results in the death of corporate (and individual) spirituality.

Our accountability to one another within the church must encompass our life in the world as witnesses of New Jerusalem. Our corporate spirituality, our nurturing of one another to wholeness in Christ for the sake of others, must include accountability for how we are seeking to be faithful to Jesus Christ in the world—in the brokenness and the dehumanizing dynamics of the community in which we live. That is an essential part of holistic spirituality.

Conclusion

We are being conformed to the image of Christ for the sake of others within the body of Christ *and* for the sake of others outside the body of Christ. Corporate spirituality and social spirituality are inseparable elements of the wholeness of our journey in faith.

The journey of faith, the path to spiritual wholeness, lies in our increasingly faithful response to the One whose purpose shapes our path, whose grace redeems our detours, whose power liberates us from the crippling bondages of our previous journey, and whose transforming presence meets us at each turn in our road. Holistic spirituality is a pilgrimage of deepening responsiveness to God's control of our life and being.

It is my prayer that you have heard God speaking to you in, through and around all that we have shared in this book. I pray that you have a clearer understanding of the spiritual journey and a hunger to enter more fully into the pilgrimage toward the wholeness in Christ that God has for you. May God richly bless you as you move forward on the journey.

Notes

Part 1: The Road Map
[1]William Ernest Henley, "Invictus," in *The Literature of England*, ed. George B. Woods et al. (Chicago: Scott, Foresman, 1958), 2:866.

Chapter 1: The Process
[1]Kenneth Leech, *Experiencing God: Theology as Spirituality* (New York: Harper & Row, 1985), p. 20.
[2]George MacDonald, "Man's Difficulty Concerning Prayer," in *Creation in Christ*, ed. Rolland Hein (Wheaton, Ill.: Harold Shaw, 1976), pp. 329-30.
[3]François Fénelon, *Christian Perfection* (Minneapolis: Dimension Books, 1975), p. 83.
[4]C. S. Lewis, *Mere Christianity* (New York: Macmillan, 1960), pp. 86-87.

Chapter 2: Being Conformed
[1]Parker Palmer, *To Know As We Are Known* (New York: Harper & Row, 1983), p. 2.
[2]*Modern Maturity*, June-July 1987, p. 13.

Chapter 3: The Image of Christ
[1]*George MacDonald: An Anthology*, ed. C. S. Lewis (New York: Macmillan, 1978), pp. 37-38.

Chapter 5: Creation Gifts
[1]I am indebted to Reginald Johnson, *Celebrate, My Soul!* (Wheaton, Ill.: Victor Books, 1988), chap. 2, for this phrase.

2For a detailed analysis of all these personality types, see Carl G. Jung, *Psychological Types* (Princeton, N.J.: Princeton University Press, 1976); David Keirsey and Marilyn Bates, *Please Understand Me: Character and Temperament Types* (Del Mar, Calif.: Prometheus Nemesis, 1978); Isabel Briggs Myers and Peter Myers, *Gifts Differing* (Palo Alto, Calif.: Consulting Psychologists Press, 1980). Especially helpful from the point of spiritual life and growth is Reginald Johnson's *Celebrate, My Soul!* (see note 1 in this chapter) and Harold Grant et al., *From Image to Likeness* (Ramsey, N.J.: Paulist, 1983).

3For a succinct description of how the preference pattern develops through our developmental stages of life, see Grant et al., *From Image to Likeness*, pp. 20-25.

4For a complete development of the model and descriptions of each pattern of preference, see Keirsey and Bates, *Please Understand Me*. For the implications of the model and its patterns for Christian spirituality, see Chester P. Michael and Marie C. Norrisey, *Prayer and Temperament: Different Prayer Forms for Different Personality Types* (Charlottesville, Va.: Open Door, 1984), as well as Johnson, *Celebrate, My Soul!*

Chapter 6: One-Sided Spirituality

1This instrument was developed by Katharine C. Briggs and Isabel Briggs Myers to help persons determine their preference pattern. Most colleges and universities with departments of psychology can administer the test. Also, there is a fairly accurate shorter instrument in Keirsey and Bates, *Please Understand Me*.

2For a fuller discussion of this aspect of the letters to the churches in Revelation, see M. Robert Mulholland Jr., *Revelation: Holy Living in an Unholy World* (Grand Rapids, Mich.: Francis Asbury, 1990).

Chapter 7: Holistic Spirituality

1Center for Applications of Psychological Type, 2815 NW 13th St., Suite 401, Gainesville, FL 32609. The charts were copyright 1981, by Earle C. Page.

2For some resources that provide guidelines for holistic spiritual practices related to our preference patterns, see Michael and Norrisey, *Prayer and Temperament*; Johnson, *Celebrate, My Soul!*; Grant et al., *From Image to Likeness*; as well as Christopher Bryant, *Prayer and Different Types of People* (Gainesville, Fla.: Center for the Application of Psychological Type, 1983).

Chapter 8: The Classical Christian Pilgrimage

1Fénelon, *Christian Perfection*, pp. 191-92.

2Benedict J. Groeschel, *Spiritual Passages* (New York: Crossroad, 1984), pp. 117-35.

[3]This study of Philippians 4:4-7 first appeared as M. Robert Mulholland Jr., "The Anatomy of Trust," *Weavings* 5 (September-October 1990): 26-32.

[4]See Herbert Preisker, "ἐπιείκεια, ἐπιεικής," in *Theological Dictionary of the New Testament,* ed. Gerhard Kittel and Gerhard Friedrich, 10 vols. (Grand Rapids, Mich.: Eerdmans, 1964-76), 2:588-90.

[5]Thomas Kelly, *A Testament of Devotion* (New York: Harper & Brothers, 1941), p. 32.

[6]Psalm 131:1-2 as found in *The Abbey Psalter: The Book of Psalms Used by the Trappist Monks of Genesee Abbey* (Ramsey, N.J.: Paulist, 1981).

[7]For a fuller explanation of the role of the elders and their worship of God in Revelation, see Mulholland, *Revelation,* pp. 155ff.

[8]Thomas Merton, *Contemplation in a World of Action* (Garden City, N.Y.: Doubleday, 1971), pp. 160-61.

[9]Groeschel, *Spiritual Passages,* p. 145.

[10]Ibid., p. 139.

[11]Adolphe Tanquerey, *The Spiritual Life: A Treatise on Ascetical and Mystical Theology,* trans. H. Branderis (Tournai, Belgium: Desclee, 1930), p. 598.

[12]Groeschel, *Spiritual Passages,* p. 161.

[13]Thomas Merton, *New Seeds of Contemplation* (Norfolk, Conn.: New Directions, 1961), pp. 4-5.

[14]Groeschel, *Spiritual Passages,* pp. 161-62.

[15]Ibid., p. 164.

[16]Ibid.

[17]Ibid., pp. 174ff.

[18]Ibid., pp. 178ff.

[19]Catherine of Genoa, *Purgation and Purgatory: The Spiritual Dialogue,* trans. S. Hughes, Classics of Western Spirituality (New York: Paulist, 1979), p. 87.

[20]Groeschel, *Spiritual Passages,* p. 179.

[21]"Absorption" is used here not in the Hindu sense of loss of self by merger into the divine, like a drop of water "absorbed" into the ocean, but in the sense of being so totally caught up in a great symphony or drama that one becomes oblivious to all except the music or action.

Chapter 9: Classical Spiritual Disciplines

[1]Richard J. Foster, *Celebration of Discipline: The Path to Spiritual Growth* (San Francisco: Harper & Row, 1978), is an excellent resource in conjunction with this section.

[2]Here are some resources on prayer that I would recommend: Anthony Bloom, *Beginning to Pray* (New York: Paulist, 1970); Anthony Bloom, *Living Prayer* (Springfield, Ill.: Templegate, 1966); Richard Foster, *Meditative Prayer* (Downers Grove, Ill.: InterVarsity Press, 1983); Kenneth Leech, *True*

Prayer (San Francisco: Harper & Row, 1980); Thomas Merton, *Contemplative Prayer* (Garden City, N.Y.: Herder and Herder, 1969); Douglas Steere, *Dimensions of Prayer* (New York: Harper & Row, 1963).

[3]Henri Nouwen, "Letting Go of All Things," *Sojourners*, May 1979, p. 6.

[4]Ibid.

[5]For a more complete discussion of the seventh seal, especially its function in the larger scope of John's vision, see Mulholland, *Revelation*, pp. 186ff.

[6]The larger development of this passage is set forth in chapter eight, "The Classical Christian Pilgrimage."

[7]In this translation of Paul's Greek, I attempt to capture the essence of Paul's use of the term usually translated "forbearance," and his expression usually translated "the Lord is near."

[8]For additional resources in this area, see a number of books by Susan A. Muto: *Approaching the Sacred: An Introduction to Spiritual Reading* (Denville, N.J.: Dimension Books, 1973); *Steps Along the Way: The Path of Spiritual Reading* (Denville, N.J.: Dimension Books, 1975); *A Practical Guide to Spiritual Reading* (Denville, N.J.: Dimension Books, 1976); *The Journey Homeward: On the Road of Spiritual Reading* (Denville, N.J.: Dimension Books, 1977); and *Renewed at Each Awakening: The Formative Power of Sacred Words* (Denville, N.J.: Dimension Books, 1979). Other resources include Thomas Merton, *Opening the Bible* (Collegeville, Minn.: Liturgical, 1970); and M. Robert Mulholland Jr., *Shaped by the Word: The Power of Scripture in Spiritual Formation* (Nashville: Upper Room, 1985).

[9]For a complete development of the contrast between informational and formational reading, see Mulholland, *Shaped by the Word*, pp. 47-60.

[10]The Latin phrase for "spiritual reading." A brief development of lectio divina can be found in M. Robert Mulholland Jr., "Spiritual Reading of Scripture," *Weavings* 3 (November-December 1988): 26-32.

[11]I am indebted to Susan A. Muto for this insight, which she shared with me during a course in spiritual reading which we team-taught at Asbury Theological Seminary in November 1986.

[12]*Wesley's Works* (Kansas City, Mo.: Beacon Hill, 1979), 14:253.

[13]As noted in chapter eight.

[14]*Wesley's Works*, 14:253.

[15]Leech, *Experiencing God*, pp. 291, 294, 296.

[16]For a succinct yet profound and holistic treatment of the discipline of fasting see Foster, *Celebration of Discipline*, chap. 4.

Chapter 10: The Nature of Spiritual Disciplines

[1]Note that "body of sin" and "might be made inoperative" are literal translations of the Greek terms in this verse.

[2]*John Wesley*, ed. Albert Outler (New York: Oxford University Press, 1964),

p. 286.
3Ibid.
4Ibid., footnote 3.
5The usual translation is "mind." The Greek word is *mind (nous)*, but in the parallelism of Romans 7:22-25, "mind" in verse 25 is parallel to "inmost being" in verse 22:

| v. 22 delight in law of God in my inmost being | v. 23 captive to law of sin |
| v. 25 serve law of God with my mind | v. 25 with my flesh serve law of sin |

6After using the Greek *nekros* for "dead" in 8:10-11, Paul now uses *thnētos*, usually translated "mortal." This is not the only place where Paul interweaves spiritual deadness with the "mortal" body. In Romans 6, after reminding us of the spiritual death *(nekros)* we have experienced in Christ (vv. 4, 9, 11), Paul exhorts us to no longer let sin reign in our "mortal" body (v. 12), since we have moved from death *(nekros)* to life (v. 13).
7This is the clear meaning of the Greek tenses.

Chapter 12: Corporate Spirituality
1Leech, *Experiencing God*, p. 22.
2Ibid. (emphasis mine).
3Ibid., p. 24.
4Ibid., p. 25.
5Most translations have something like "Jesus did not trust [or entrust] himself to them." But in the Greek it is the exact same word in both places: "Many believed *[pisteuō]* in Jesus. . . . Jesus did not believe *[pisteuō]* himself to them."
6The reason for using noninclusive language here will be evident in a moment.
7In John's Greek, as in the Aramaic Jesus most likely would have spoken to Nicodemus, the word for "spirit" and the word for "wind" are the same. We lose the wordplay in English.

Chapter 13: Social Spirituality
1Leech, *Experiencing God*, p. 381.
2Ibid., p. 379.
3Ibid., p. 384.
4Ibid., p. 391.
5For a full treatment of Revelation in this perspective, see Mulholland, *Revelation*.
6Leech, *Experiencing God*, p. 380.